PRAISE FOR

From Shy To Social

"Engaging, well-researched and frequently hilarious, *From Shy To Social* is one of those rare self-help books that feels like you're being coached and encouraged by a trusted friend. An absolute must-read for all of the love shy men out there."
– Sofi Papamarko, Relationship Columnist & Contributor to *The Huffington Post* and *The Globe & Mail*

"This is an important topic that affects so many men, who will be happy to have this book!"
– Liza Fromer, host of *The Morning Show, Global TV*

"While many men dream about success with dating, the truly motivated do everything possible to make that happen. Former 'shy guy' author Christopher Gray embarked on a journey to develop his skill at relating to others, and shares his insights in this valuable guide to boosting your self-confidence and ability to develop both social and romantic relationships. Unlike a lot of people who write about relationships, Chris doesn't just offer conversational tips and tricks for attracting interest from women – he can help you develop a better self-image and strategies for attracting the women you want."
– Kateryna Spiwak, Professional Dating & Relationship Coach

"The best counsel always comes from personal experience and in *From Shy To Social: The Shy Man's Guide to Personal & Dating Success,* Christopher Gray's life-long journey through shyness is an outstanding resource which will resonate deeply for any man who struggles with a need for love and connection and the realities of being shy."
– Dale Curd, Counselor, Men's Issues Expert & host of *Guy Talk, CFRB Radio*

From Shy To Social:

The
SHY MAN'S GUIDE
To
PERSONAL
&
DATING SUCCESS

Christopher Gray

Sunbow Press

TORONTO

ISBN: 978-0-9868364-2-8

Library and Archives Canada Cataloguing in Publication

Gray, Christopher [date]
    From shy to social : the shy man's guide to personal & dating
success / Christopher Gray.

Includes bibliographical references and index.
Issued also in electronic format under ISBN 978-0-9868364-1-1.

ISBN 978-0-9868364-2-8

    1. Dating (Social customs). 2. Bashfulness. 3. Man-woman relationships.
I. Title.

HQ801.G698 2011   646.7'7   C2011-905904-5

For shy people everywhere

*...and the Mothers & Fathers who
wish their sons happiness in life*

Contents

Preface   1

Introduction   3

1 Understanding Shyness   7

What's Holding You Back?   19

Negative versus Positive Thoughts   29

2 Be Proactive: Chart a New Direction   36

Lifestyle Choices that Lead to Misery   44

Emerging from your Seclusion, one step at a time   45

Assignment #1: Online Contributions   48

Working on your Voice   49

Assignment #2: Voice & Telephone Clarity   54

Personal Grooming   55

Develop some Style   56

Body Language & Posture   59

Assignment #3: Improve your Look   65

What is your Daily Routine?   67

3 Getting used to Interacting with People   72

Assignment #4: Saying "Hello" to Strangers   74

Assignment #5: Short Conversations with Strangers   76

Assignment #6: Enroll in Special Interest Courses   77

4 The Art of Conversation   80

How to Get Invited to Parties   87

Building your Social Proof   91

Don't be a Cheapskate   92

5 What Women Want   94

Why Women Like Bad Boys   97

ASSIGNMENT #7: APPROACH 50 WOMEN IN 10 DAYS   104

   WHERE TO ENGAGE WITH WOMEN (EXTENDED DURATION)   106

   ONLINE DATING   114

   SPEED DATING   119

6 PICKUP ARTISTS   120

7 PUTTING THEORIES INTO PRACTICE   130

   WHERE TO ENGAGE WITH WOMEN (FLEETING DURATION)   132

ASSIGNMENT #8: APPROACHES LEADING TO CONVERSATION   139

8 APPROACHING IN BARS AND CLUBS   142

   SWITCHING FROM THE OPENER TO CONVERSATION   147

9 DAYTIME APPROACHES   152

   REDUCING THE FLAKE-OUT FACTOR   163

   LIMITING BELIEFS WITH APPROACHES   166

10 THEORY VERSUS REALITY   171

   APPROACH ANXIETY   177

   SOLUTIONS TO APPROACH ROADBLOCKS   182

   BEFORE YOUR DATE: PHONE GAME   183

11 WHEN ON A DATE   184

12 ENSURING YOU GET A SECOND DATE   189

FINAL ASSIGNMENT   201

PREFACE

I struggled with social anxiety disorder and an almost debilitating lack of confidence for many years. Through extensive research, interviews with psychologists and behavioral experts, experimentation and trial & error, I managed to conquer my social phobias and create a rich, satisfying social life. This book is designed to help the shy guy's dating situation through the benefit of my own experience and solutions.

This semi-autobiographical journey is essentially divided into two parts – the first deals with reducing anxiety and shyness so that you can comfortably interact with others, and then we switch over to the male-female dynamic in which approach and conversation skills with women is addressed, with the aim of creating a healthy dating life. This book is a comprehensive plan detailing the methods I used to change from being extremely self-conscious around women I was interested in, to someone who could confidently initiate conversation with women under almost any conditions, concurrent with a far richer social life.

My research consisted of consultation with experts and their material in the fields of attraction, psychology, social science and the arts. Some of these include dating & lifestyle coaches Kateryna Spiwak and Michael Marks, the writings of Joseph O'Connor & John Seymour in their book *Introducing NLP,* Michael Ellsberg's *The Power of Eye Contact,* Michael Pilinski's *Without Embarrassment,* Richard Machowicz's *Unleash The Warrior Within;* attraction experts Neil Strauss' *The Rules of The Game,*

Mystery's *The Mystery Method*, the writings of social etiquette expert Leil Lowndes, and other works in various fields. Also of note are the teachers at Second City Improv and The Bad Dog Theatre Company in Toronto, who are consistently able to instruct their students in the skill of on-the-spot conversation while being funny at the same time.

The result of my efforts is a proven program of self-improvement which will help you eliminate the shyness or lack of self-esteem or lack of confidence that may be holding you back. You will become the better man you want to be, while opening up new social avenues for meeting women.

I am about to change your life for the better.

INTRODUCTION

It was just before Christmas 2005 and I was wandering through a grocery store, out of a relationship, feeling very depressed. I had tried online dating without much success. I wanted to be in a new relationship, but felt powerless to meet women, let alone ask one out for a date.

I saw a woman carrying a shopping basket; we passed each other in the aisle, glancing at one another. I continued shopping but made my way back towards where I thought she'd be. I didn't see her, so thinking she had left I made my way to the checkout. As luck would have it, she was in line, and I moved in just after her. I took note of what was in her basket; there were lots of vegetables, and other healthy choices. Despite my nervousness at the prospect, I decided to initiate conversation: "You sure eat with nutrition in mind."

She smiled. "Thanks, but you caught me on a good day, I might just as well have had some chocolate and frozen food instead, but I wanted to eat better before all the holiday deserts started."

"Have you done all of your gift shopping?" I asked. "Just one or two more people to buy for," she replied, as she finished paying for her groceries. Now my items were being rung through. I wanted to get her number, or give her mine. But damn, she was starting to leave, the cashier was there and would hear my attempt. My heart was pounding, and I was starting to panic, unsure of what to do next. "Well, happy holidays," she said, as she walked away.

And she disappeared. As my items were being bagged, I saw her pass by the window outside, and she briefly glanced at me. A moment later I paid for my groceries and hurried out, hoping to catch her and ask for her number. But she was gone.

I returned to that store many times hoping to see her. Although I have dated many women since then, I will always look upon that moment as a tragic lost opportunity, wondering how things might have turned out had I seized it.

I vowed to never let something like that happen again.

It's a true story and a common scenario for many men, especially those who are shy (or *extremely reserved,* as some prefer to call the condition). There's nothing more frustrating for a guy to have this feeling of helplessness, to literally watch an attractive woman slip by, and not know how to fix the situation. Sure, there is always the standard advice of *just go for it,* but if you don't have the skills, your fear gets in the way, sabotaging your approach – if you can approach at all.

Most of us believe women do not want to be approached by guys, because we think it would be obvious we were hitting on her. So we wait until conditions are absolutely perfect. The trouble is, if you are shy the perfect conditions are about as common as a grand-prize lottery win.

For many reserved guys, dating is a cruel exercise in failure. For myself it was only after many years of repetitive frustration that I finally chose to chart a new destiny and improve my situation; the alternative was absolutely horrifying: stay in the same rut, have zero success with women, and die alone surrounded by cute but unappreciative goldfish. At first I was clueless about how to fix the situation. Then I went looking for answers, which I have detailed here.

Though we examine actual conversations with women that led to dates, this is not a Pickup Artist (PUA) book, but neither is it simply a manual that only targets your social anxiety. I wanted to produce a well-rounded, one-stop program, one that would tackle this frustrating dating problem for guys everywhere, no matter their age or social comfort level.

As someone who has been there and then found pathways to success, I am going to outline a series of exercises and instructions designed to improve your social skills, measure by measure, until you are able to function at a level far beyond what you now experience.

I've included sections on the different social behavior of men and women, theories on attraction, and practical assignments designed to help the extremely reserved man evolve from a stammering recluse into a confident man who is comfortable interacting fully with women in whom he is interested.

I also researched the sometimes locked-in defeatist mindsets that some men with social anxiety employ (the depth and extent of those defeatist mindsets and negative convictions may surprise you), and the common tendency to blame others rather than put in the effort and practice the techniques and habits needed to improve their lives.

Later in the book I analyze for you the latest introduction techniques and how shy men can learn to apply them effectively.

Included are many examples of actual opening lines and conversations that have led to dates to give you a clear understanding about the nature of attraction, and how to apply it all to achieve successful dating.

Going from being extremely shy to comfortably interacting with women may seem like a very ambitious goal to some. Much of my progress was trial and error, and it took years to reach my present level of confidence in social situations and having engaging conversations with women I find attractive. My aim is to not only give the reader a deeper understanding of the problem of shyness as it relates to dating, but offer tips, insight and reference-style assignments that will reduce the total time investment to a fraction of what it would otherwise take.

One

UNDERSTANDING SHYNESS

As shy individuals, we face an uphill battle. The world is awash with competition and ambition, in everything from getting a job to getting a date. If you are a reserved individual and hesitate or fail to convince others of your positive attributes there will always be someone else ready to take what could be yours. This is true everywhere – with recreational sports teams, the workplace, and especially dating.

Every year thousands of articles and books are published on dating and relationships. Suggestions are given on where to go to meet women, how to ask a woman out, cultivating your bad boy attitude to make women swoon, and so on. The vast majority of these self-help sources assume the reader just needs a little tweaking in their presentation to get their dating engine started.

Unfortunately for the love shy, the advice these books espouse is completely useless.

Love shy people, especially shy men, are so far removed from a healthy dating life that the simple "polish" or "attitude adjustment" as preached by some guides is about as effective as trying to paddle up Niagara Falls.

In fact, most self-help relationship books pay only scant attention to the love shy, if the topic is mentioned at all. One relationship book I read devoted a single paragraph to the extremely shy; the author had little to offer, suggesting reserved, awkward daters with low self-esteem seek counseling for any deep-seated trauma before attempting to date. While this may be sound advice for those with deep-seated trauma, it is of little benefit to the just plain shy.

I have taken a more realistic approach with this book, which is designed expressly for the Love Shy Man – a particularly difficult dater whose overriding lack of confidence affects every aspect of his life, and all but completely ensures his prior dating prospects were nil.

I say "his" life because overall this tends to be more of a male problem. In general terms it is the man that is expected to take the assertive role, in everything from the initial approach, to the first kiss, and finally the act of sex itself. This is a generalization but gender roles bear this out, something I have seen in my own personal experience, although there is a cultural shift afoot where women feel comfortable in asking a man out.

Not to minimize the suffering some shy women go through, but given their allowed passivity in the dating world women don't need to be as outgoing to attract men (although the extremely shy, reclusive woman will of course have just as difficult a time of it; even though written from a male perspective, following the exercises in this book will help). Being shy romantically is generally worse for guys – women are less likely to interact with a reserved, awkward man who finds small talk difficult.

That's not to say there are not sexually assertive women out there – as there most certainly are – those who may help move things along if they happen to be interested in a male that is a little slow to progress things romantically, in effect introducing him to adult relationships. But even a sexually assertive woman can't help the man that is so painfully shy he hardly meets or speaks to anyone.

It will take time and effort. But what worth doing in life doesn't? How many hours of court time does a beginner-recreational tennis player need in order to win matches with better players? How much classroom and research time does it take to upgrade your education? How long does it take to become fluent in another language?

All of these activities contribute to the richness of the participant's life. The tennis player gets to keep fit and spend time with friends in a sport he enjoys. The college graduate has an education that will help him find the career he wants. And the language student is able to live and work abroad with far greater ease. The alternative – to not make the effort at self-improvement – is to stagnate.

Mastering any of these goals is not easy, yet people undertake them all the time. They put in the necessary effort to attain those goals to improve their lives. And once they reach a certain level, it becomes far easier – the sports enthusiast requires less practice to maintain his game; the graduate has the educational foundation to further his career; the person with a second language under his belt can maintain his fluency with semi-regular interaction with native speakers.

You will notice the same thing with your social skills. You will experience breakthroughs, small and large, until you have reached a point where your friends hardly recognize the person you have become. A currently terrifying activity (such as giving a public speech or asking a woman out) will become relatively easy. You may never completely eradicate feelings of unease, but instead of keeping you down, those feelings will only motivate you to do well.

Up to now you have not had a lot of success with women. Unlike the progress that most people make in the march to adulthood, your insecurities may be just as strong now as when you were a teen, and are preventing you from enjoying your life. I have some good news for you:

- **It isn't entirely your fault**
- **You can improve to a level you never thought possible**

Sound promising? If you are like me, you have made more than a few excuses for the failures in your life. Maybe you blame circumstance, your upbringing, your loser friends that drag you down, your astrological sign, or you just plain think all women are not very nice. If you've gotten past that stage and have realized you have a distinct lack of confidence and poise that prevents you from making progress in social situations (dating or professional), congratulations, you have taken the first step to improving your life.

The Desire to be Sociable

I used to loath the idea of going out and socializing, because I was so uncomfortable around people and was depressed because of what I felt was my awful lot in life, to be insecure and reserved to the point of having a hard time in social situations, to say nothing of dating. Even though I was never diagnosed as clinically depressed, I was often very unhappy, as a teen locking myself away in my room to stew in despair.

Even as a young adult my natural progress was glacially slow. Sure, life experience was making me a little more sociable each year, but at the rate I was going I would be comfortable around women sometime around my hundredth birthday. I was miserable and could see no way out. Something had to be done.

Finally realizing most people were decent and even friendly if I was relaxed and open to talking, helped me work towards overcoming my pessimistic outlook. Over and above that was the realization that despite all the wars and crime in the world, we live in a generally decent society where most people are just trying to live their lives in peace and have a few good times along the way.

One of the first major changes I experienced was while at university, when a room mate who was working on a campus handbook offered me a job as the advertising salesperson. She didn't offer it to me because she thought I would be particularly good at it, but because nobody else wanted the job.

This turned out to be a stroke of luck because it allowed me to engage with customers in a non-social context, which took a lot of the pressure off in my interactions with people. I didn't need to be entertaining and I had no fear of being boring. I was there to do a job (sell them advertising), and because I believed it was a good deal for the customer, I was able to be sincere and engaging in all my interactions.

I did well, and my success led to a similar job with the campus newspaper. This was another great job in that I got to know the staff (editors, writers, layout artists, etc.) in a very friendly environment, even though I was still extremely reserved and didn't socialize much with the other employees. Probably 60% of the staff were women.

And this had a happy outcome. One of the female volunteers at the paper took a liking to me, seducing me in short order. She was my first 'real' girlfriend, and we were together for the rest of the semester. Unfortunately she ended up cheating on me and our relationship ended, largely because I lacked the emotional intelligence to keep it going – not having much prior contact with women in a romantic context meant I was not good at recognizing what women need and want in a relationship.

But hey, that's sometimes life on campus; relationships can be fleeting, so I didn't take it that hard. You'd think that this experience of having a girlfriend would have quickly led to further relationships, but you'd be wrong. It turns out the seduction I experienced was more of a fluke than an indication of what was in store as I ventured into the real world.

The advertising job while at university was a great social catalyst, but my health took a turn for the worse as I developed Chronic Fatigue Syndrome (CFS), and was unable to go out much for a few years. My lack of confidence and quiet nature continued, and with the exception of a couple of one night stands, I would not have another fulfilling relationship for several years.

CFS put a damper on my social life for a number of years, and after I more or less recovered, I suffered a prolonged period of loneliness due to my own inaction. Yes, I did go on a couple of blind dates set up by friends, and I did manage to snag a few dates from online sites, but nothing went beyond the first date. The most likely cause was my behavior; due to my shyness I was extremely reserved, and came across as boring and uncomfortable. Secondly, besides my job, I was doing absolutely nothing with my life. No outside interests, no fitness regimen, and I attended few social events.

Part of the problem was the aforementioned CFS, which delayed my social progress. But I must be honest here. Even during my recovery I wasn't doing much to improve my situation. Had I taken charge of my life sooner, I wouldn't have had so many years of boredom and loneliness.

Genetics, Environment, or Both?

As with some other psychological conditions there is a genetic component to shyness. With so many mood disorders afflicting people it has been suggested by some experts that they are an evolutionary adaptation, with shyness and depression possibly helping the individual survive by preventing them from taking excessively dangerous risks.[1] Unfortunately this adaptation can be a hindrance when it comes to finding a mate.

If social anxiety disorder runs in families there is enough genetic variation to ensure not every child of shy parents is shy themselves, just as a blue-eyed child can be born to parents with brown eyes (provided both parents carry the blue recessive gene).

Of course there is an impact from upbringing as well. Reserved, quiet parents are less likely to produce a child that grows up to be a hell raiser (but it can happen, as can the reverse). My parents were both outgoing, yet I (alone among the three siblings) was always quite reserved. My maternal Grandfather was very shy; this genetic trait was likely passed on to me.

I believe genetics is the primary explanation for most people's shyness. Nevertheless, there are possibly dozens of potential environmental factors as well, mostly occurring during childhood, such as:

- Bullying or excessive ridicule
- Parents that discouraged independence or dissension
- Traumatic events

And countless other causes. If you were confronted by an extremely acute childhood trauma that is unduly affecting you in adulthood, it is probably best that you seek professional help. Such scenarios are beyond the scope of this book. In other words, I can't help you if being abducted and smacked around by meth-addicted lingerie models at the age of thirteen has affected your outlook towards attractive women. However, this book is designed to be used as a guide to help you overcome your social anxiety and improve your social life, especially with women.

Three Degrees of Shyness

Let's take stock of the realities of your social life. If you are only slightly reserved you may be making a genuine effort to get out there and meet people, yet still have a debilitating confidence problem. In this case you can concentrate on your outlook and methodology, and (with the help of the assignments in later chapters) will be well on your way to improving your dating life.

On the other hand, if you are very dissatisfied with your present state and have an underdeveloped social life, few friends, and hold out little hope for a positive change, we will identify what the stumbling blocks are and work on a program of improving your situation. I have identified three degrees of shyness: the *Recluse*, the *Shy Pessimist*, and the *Shy Optimist*.

The Recluse

When this person finishes work, they go home and watch television or surf the internet. That is, if they have a job to come home from – some guys are so stuck in a rut they may be unemployed and living with their parents, with no apparent way out. I'm not knocking people that may be victims of a recession and have had to temporarily move back in with relatives; I'm referring to guys that have a decent education, are able to work, but who are so afraid of getting out into the world they still live with their parents sometimes well into their thirties or even forties.

The Recluse is a slave to the routine of staying home. He does not have any outside interests (besides surfing the internet), has few (if any) friends, and may experience extreme unease even when interacting with relatives other than his parents or siblings. Fear and resignation are the key words here – fear of going out and exploring the world, fear of social rejection (not just by women, but by the general public), and a resignation that the situation will not improve. There is a comfort level they have built for themselves, and it does not involve making the effort to change. Thus, it is difficult for the recluse to make social progress.

The life of the recluse can be bettered, but the person will usually need a concerned relative to give them a push in the right direction since they are unlikely to take the first step in self-improvement on their own (such as going out and buying this book).

The Shy Pessimist

This person has friends, but they are few in number and mostly old friends from school. He generally does not hang out in a group, but rather has made friends on an individual basis. Like the Recluse, the Shy Pessimist has such a negative view of himself he is unlikely to partake in many social activities on his own. But in contrast to the former, this person may be dragged out of the house by a friend for the occasional social outing.

However, he has basically resigned himself to the misery of having a continuously poor track record with women.

The Shy Pessimist's biggest enemy is his negative self-image, which in some cases can be even worse than that of the Recluse who is more likely to have resigned himself to a safe, uneventful routine. The Shy Pessimist looks upon outgoing people with envy, longing to be accepted into a larger social circle, but he may also cling to the mistaken belief that people and society are to blame for most of his problems. Much energy and time is spent stewing in their plight, while feeling powerless to enact change.

The Shy Pessimist usually has difficulty talking to most women, even those he is not romantically interested in. A comfortable routine of staying indoors is tempting; besides the occasional outing with persistent friends, the Shy Pessimist may also be prodded by concerned relatives. But to improve he must take it upon himself to make the effort. He will have a slightly easier time of it than the Recluse, perhaps by getting so fed up with his plight that he goes looking for a solution.

The Shy Optimist

Compared to those in the other two groups, the Shy Optimist doesn't tend to blame society for his problems and has a fairly rich social life, at least among friends and coworkers. He is willing and able to partake in outside interests, and sometimes initiates social outings among peer groups. He can usually talk to women he's not romantically interest in, but has an overriding fear of interacting with women he is attracted to, so he rarely dates or is rarely able to get a second date, due to being nervous or coming across as uninteresting.

When he reaches a point at which he feels his natural progress is at a standstill, he will actively look for courses, books, advisors and other means to improve his dating skills. Being the most open minded and likely to seek solutions, the Shy Optimist is very keen to improve his situation and has the greatest chance of success.

Some of us Weren't Shy as Children

Some reserved people were shy at an extremely early age. Others become reclusive as they enter their teens. Ever notice that most children, from about the age of three to eight, are the most fearless talkers? They will happily tell you about their day, the funny things their classmates said, the interesting things they saw on their way from school, and how they are feeling now. That's because they have not yet been completely discouraged by the concept of making fools of themselves. As they approach the age of ten and greater, they become aware of other people's social missteps and their consequences (ridicule from others). It is at this point many children become self-conscious. Some become withdrawn, greatly curtailing their former exuberance.

At no time is this more prevalent than during the teen years, when social acceptance is at its most important. For many of us, this is the time we suddenly clam up. Some people never regain their childhood fearlessness. But in addition to being more cognizant of social acceptance and rejection in others, this is the age at which we go through puberty, a time of many bodily and hormonal changes that can affect our personality.

In fact there are so many physiological changes going on during the transition from child to adult it is no surprise that so many young people experience mood disorders including depression, bipolar disorder, and other ailments that affect their psychological well-being and interactions with others. Some of these difficulties can be dealt with through expert counseling.

Support networks for social anxiety can be found on the web these days, but It can still be difficult for both the sufferer and the parents to adequately communicate about the issue, let alone deal with it. Upon seeing their child or teenager struggling with shyness, parents will naturally express their concern. However, it is embarrassing for the sufferer who may reply to any questioning with stilted non-answers or vagaries because he is uncomfortable. And parents who are socially proficient themselves may have difficulty relating to extreme social anxiety, asking the wrong questions and proposing simplistic, unrealistic solutions such as *try to be more outgoing.*

The relatives of a shy teen might push him into social situations he wasn't ready for, such as sending him to a community event where he will be expected to interact with people of similar age he had never seen before, most of whom would already belong to an established peer group. This is like pushing a non-swimmer into the deep end of a pool and expecting them to naturally tread water, rather than flail about in a panic. Occasionally it works; most of the time it doesn't.

Despite the kind intent, pushing a non-swimmer into the deep end does not teach the person to swim or make them more comfortable in deep water; on the contrary, even for those few who don't need to be hauled spluttering and flailing out of the pool or lake, it can increase their fear. A better strategy for social conditioning is to regularly introduce them to less stressful social settings, as with a smaller group in a familiar environment. Just as with learning to swim, the whole successful process begins with small steps.

While pushing the shy teen into the deep end is not advised, neither is coddling or shielding them from social interaction. A balance must be struck, where the person can be introduced to new social interactions on a gradual basis. This can include enrolling them into small arts and drama classes, special interest clubs, and even special programs (if they are available in your area) that are designed for the extremely shy.

For some shy men, solutions come naturally with age and experience, but that is a poor consolation for someone who presently suffers from social anxiety. Few of us want to bide our time for ten or twenty years before being able to achieve successful, satisfying and happy relationships and social interactions. We want and deserve those things now.

In Society, Shy People are Second Class

Think of any exuberant, extroverted and funny people that you know presently. Chances are, they are very popular, make people laugh, and have many friends. These people aren't afraid of what others think. Note that I'm talking about well-adjusted, fair-minded jokesters, not mean-spirited sociopaths. The majority of people that witness or are included in fun behavior with such characters don't judge such behavior as stupid – something they might have done when they were young and insecure.

Quite the opposite, they embrace it because of the feel-good moment it brings.

Though it may be difficult for you to understand the power of a positive mindset at this early stage, my point here is that most of us are too afraid to let loose, by telling a joke, engaging in conversation with someone we hardly know, or letting our opinion be known. This social phobia greatly reduces the fun factor in life, leading to needless loneliness and misery.

Obviously, the solution is not as simple as someone's ill-conceived suggestion to "loosen up and tell more jokes." However, that is the general effect we are aiming for over time, and there are many exercises we will engage in to set us on that path.

Dating and mating behaviors are learned. They are complex social skills, which for most involve many failures before any success is realized. Yet for some reason society thinks dating is a natural process that we should get right, without much guidance. As a result, we are left to stumble through the process while our nervously hopeful parents cross their fingers that we will find 'the one.'

Cultural norms fail us badly here. The only social items taught in my big-city high school concerning the opposite sex were square dancing and the dangers of sexually transmitted diseases. Square dancing. Can you believe it? Before you think I went to school in the Dark Ages, this was on the school board's educational curriculum into the 1980s – about when Michael Jackson was teaching us the Moon Walk.

Were there any social etiquette classes at your high school? Were there any coaches to give you tips on how to ask a girl out? Most of our acquaintences and relatives offered only the standard advice to *just be yourself and the rest will come naturally*. Arrgh!

Dating requires learning complex social rules, reading subtle body language which often contradicts what the person is saying verbally, and experiencing rejection, often without knowing what we did wrong. As if that weren't enough, there is competition among the players for relationships with the most desirable women. If you hesitate, you lose.

Further, males and females are wired differently when it comes to social interactions. Women are more verbally and emotionally expressive, but they also tend to pick up on non-verbal communication better than men. Being nervous or insecure can destroy your chances with a woman even before you utter a single word to her.

If you are even mildly socially inept things get really difficult. If you are love shy, the obstacles increase exponentially.

Just be Yourself? (The phrase we all hate!)

How many times have you heard this phrase: *Just be yourself and you'll do fine.*

That is a very irritating piece of advice, but is at the same time a valid concept. Many men with social anxiety learn to hate the phrase because it flows trippingly from the mouths of so many well-meaning advice givers who have no clue that you'd love to be able to just be yourself *right this very minute.* Like we've never heard that before. It's yet another main reason I wrote this book.

The phrase is foolhardy because it assumes we are able to put forward our best self at any given moment, for any important interaction, date, job interview, etc. But take a moment to think about how often our best self is on the scene.

Let's assume most of your social interactions are awkward, stressful, and short. But there is probably one person with whom you feel comfortable – a sibling, cousin, childhood friend – and with whom you are able to joke around, have intense conversations, and just plain relax. This is the person that sees your best self; the interesting, funny, energetic guy who is fun to talk to.

As soon as you encounter someone else – let's say other distant relatives with whom you feel less comfortable, an acquaintance, coworker, or stranger – you are your usual reserved self, looking pensive, without much of anything interesting to say.

So for that time you spend with those one or two people you feel very comfortable with – perhaps 1% of your conscious time – you are at your best. And the difference between your best self and your usual, stammering self is huge.

Now let's look at the typical guy – not necessarily the super-popular valedictorian from your high school, but the average guy that is able to date without too much difficulty, has a fair number of friends, and a good

Stopping the glitch.

job. How much of his conscious time is devoted to putting his best self forward?

Probably not a lot more than you, and yet he is successful in gaining friends and women. How is that?

This typical guy is not extremely self-conscious, and so the difference between his best and usual self is not that great. In simple terms, the distinction between you and the typical guy is the *spread* between your "best" and "usual" selves – expansive for you, much less so for him, because of his relatively high comfort level. We will work to narrow that difference; we'll keep and improve upon your best self, while raising the bar on your usual self.

What's Holding You Back?

If you have not had much success with women (or with anyone else in social circumstances), you've probably spent a lot of time analyzing the situation. Some shy men blame themselves, others blame society, others blame women in general. These are misconceptions and limiting beliefs that are difficult to change, but which must change if you are to successfully move forward.

The most common difficulty a shy person faces is feeling inferior but there are also those who exhibit a superiority complex. Occasionally both conditions are present. Either of these will negatively influence your personality and thus hinder your interpersonal relationships.

Inferiority Complex

Among all shy people, there is a common denominator: low self esteem. Even the *Shy Optimist* can suffer from this, which often involves self-recrimination for being reserved around women to whom you're attracted. The inferiority complex can range from a mild lack of confidence to an overwhelming feeling that everyone else on the planet is better than you are.

If you belong to one of the first two groups *(Recluse or Shy Pessimist),* you likely have the following thoughts regularly:

- People find me uninteresting
- I am not an easy person to get to know
- I have nothing to contribute to the group
- Women find me unattractive

The common theme here is a feeling of low self-worth. I'm sure you have experienced the usual pep talk from a relative, where they say something like *hang in there, you'll find someone.* How do you react? Your thoughts probably include:

- It's not worth the effort, I've been miserable my whole life
- People can't change who they are, so I'm doomed to stay loveless

These are common thoughts among the socially awkward. It's easy for someone to come along and say, *shape up, get out of that funk; smile; don't be so shy.* Right. If you've ever been extremely shy, those words grate like few others.

It is easy to feel inferior when you see a confident person operate, someone that stands out from the crowd. Such a person is usually direct, is able to converse with ease, is effortlessly humorous, and as a result has a great job, many friends, and gets a lot of attention from women.

That isn't to say the confident person's reality completely matches the persona they project. They may have many hidden, nagging fears, such as being worried about making their house payments; they may have problems at home with their partner; they may be experiencing regret at their direction in life, and many other self-doubts that dominate their thoughts when they are alone.

Here's the truth: *most people are not better than you.* Almost everyone has some insecurities and social fears of one sort or another. Those who are able to minimize them and work through them excel in social situations. The fully self-actualized person who has reached a level of self-security that allows him to live his life free of baggage, fear, hesitation and self-doubt is extremely rare.

That does not mean you should not strive to be such a person. In fact, that should be your goal – to reach a point in your social condition and outlook in which you are able to function in any situation with confidence, and no longer constantly worry or care what other people think.

Society tends to pick a few people above others to worship, and not necessarily for their integrity or generosity. Celebrities are perfect examples: pop stars, internet personalities, famous musicians, movie actors. They haven't cured any diseases or brought world peace. Through hard work, talent and a little luck they've achieved notice, and reap the benefits (and curses) of recognition, notoriety, adulation and attention. Newspapers, magazines, TV shows and web bloggers clamor to interview them. Photographers stake out their houses to photograph them. All because the public has been taught to adore or revile or become somehow fascinated by them.

Meanwhile, in their private lives, they are just like us and often far worse. How many stars have been to rehab, have been charged with drunk driving, were left by their spouse, etc. These people are not better than you are; never forget that.

The immensely talented Meryl Streep has been quoted many times about the inherent and sometimes insurmountable insecurity she's experienced stating that *"I fear one day I'll wake up to find that everyone has finally realized I'm a talentless nobody who has been fooling them all these years."* Ms. Streep lives with the same self-doubt as us, but her success shows that she doesn't let her negative thoughts dominate her life.

Superiority Complex and the Nice Guy Myth

The other side of the coin is a superiority complex. How can a shy person have a superiority complex, you may ask? This can manifest if they constantly blame others for their lack of social success while taking little responsibility themselves. It isn't necessary to be male or have social anxiety to exhibit this personality characteristic, but some shy guys definitely fit into this category.

The 'nice guy' may look upon himself as having better morals than most people, especially if he sees those he thinks are jerks getting promoted at work and having more success with women. Or he may think society as a whole is at fault, for promoting competition and letting the unscrupulous go unpunished (or rewarded for being bold) while he, a meek, yet *good* guy, stays put.

Sometimes society does seem to be blind, occasionally letting the charismatic get away with transgressions that would normally result in punishment for the average person. Since society is comprised of imperfect individuals, society itself is imperfect. You must come to terms with this fact unless you decide to go live in a cave somewhere.

Blaming society and the people you associate with for your lack of happiness only leads to more failure. Choosing to believe others are responsible for your situation or that society is biased or made up of corrupt individuals, is an extremist, defeatist exercise that will not change your condition. You may think to yourself, *"the people around me and society as a whole combine to defeat my best efforts."* Those who subscribe to this view never quite understand that the true cause of the problem is their unwillingness to address their undeveloped social skills.

And I hate to break it to you, but if you experience some of this bitterness and consider yourself to be a nice guy, you are probably nowhere near as nice as you think. The nice guy's overly considerate nature is to some extent a false persona, *unconsciously* crafted as a tool to facilitate his desires. Pilinski goes as far as to say that the self-proclaimed 'nice guy' is in fact angry, selfish, emotionally demanding and manipulative due to his feelings of insecurity, an exaggerated sense of injustice, and simmering frustration as his desires go unfulfilled.[2]

Although most of us are capable of altruistic behavior (putting other's needs ahead of our own, taking care of a person in need, etc.), we are only human. Beyond the basic requirements of food, shelter and security, we all have selfish desires: a prestigious job, social status, influence over others, money, and attention from those we find attractive. People employ different methods in the attempt to procure what they want.

Some people fulfill their desires through a solid work ethic and an adventurous spirit, being sociable and assertive or perhaps charmingly persuasive. Other, less charismatic or industrious people have less success and may be envious of those who are. The meek person does not feel he has tools such as sociability and the drive to take moderate risks, and so employs amiable nice guy behavior as a means to succeed. This can apply in all aspects of life, not just the romantic or relationship quest.

By being agreeable in most situations, the nice guy hopes he will get the things he desires, such as a promotion at work and a date with the

beautiful woman he sits next to in evening class. Unfortunately, a habitu-
ally agreeable nature is not seen as high status, and so employers tend to
promote the go-getter who will get the job done over the nice guy who
may not be as charismatic.

Similarly, a woman can be treated wonderfully by the nice guy who
listens to her complaints about her boyfriend and agrees with almost
everything she says. She appreciates him as a friend, but sees absolutely
no romantic potential in the nice guy, because he has not stepped up with
any of the traits of assertiveness, confidence, authority and strength that
women look for in a partner.

In each case, the nice behavior is a tactic to get what he wants, and
when it doesn't work he fumes over the injustice, thinking people should
appreciate how nice and upstanding he is, and they are ignorant, superficial jerks if they do not.

Even if you are starting to recognize this situation in yourself, you may
still cling to the belief that you are truly a nice person with no hidden
agenda. Test yourself here.

- Are you as pleasant to a woman you consider physically unattractive compared to the women you normally drool over? Nope – the less attractive
  woman doesn't appeal to you so you barely acknowledge her. Or, maybe you
  are feeling charitable and make small talk, but the instant she shows you
  any romantic interest, you turn away. You want something from a beautiful
  woman and being extra nice is your hopeful strategy to somehow hook up
  with her. Despite your nice guy persona, in this scenario your motives are no
  better than anyone else's (even those of the jerks you despise).

- Do you find yourself getting bitterly disappointed and angry with friends or
  family if they don't do things you ask of them, especially if you have been
  nice? Do you think that if they truly cared about you, they would do the task
  or favor you ask, and since you were so considerate to them earlier they now
  have an obligation to you? Your friends are probably willing to help you in
  most areas, but if what you want falls under matters of opinion they may not
  agree or regard the issue as importantly. True integrity means that you're
  capable of accepting the independence, failures, differences and even the
  thoughtlessness of others. People have independent lives and goals. Some

will disappoint you, as you will disappoint others from time to time. Being a nice guy means defining what you truly believe are the best ways to conduct yourself and yourself alone. It has nothing to do with what others do.

- Do you often make helpful suggestions to friends or family on how they should be doing something, and then if they don't follow your advice, feel they are doing so just to spite you or are being ignorant? Know that the best way to offer advice or guidance to others is by living your life in a way that others will want to emulate, not by pushing them to do things your way. Again, people have independent goals; few will do as you suggest and fewer still will do what you repeatedly or strongly advise them to do no matter how well-intentioned your words. Being a nice person means being the one people refer to when a decision of some sort is being considered, not getting resentful or criticizing them if their actions don't follow your 'guidance.'

If any of the above examples are true, your considerate nature is largely due to a desire for control and is a leveraging tool to get what you want.

For some men this nice guy paradox is quite serious, extending beyond the romantic into most of his interactions. In such cases he may think his position is unassailable, while everyone else is ignorant and uncooperative. Rationalization is common, where he looks upon other people as wrong (or bad), and himself as right (or good), and so he refuses to put much stock in other points of view should they conflict with his own.

The nice guy's feelings are easily hurt which puts an additional burden on those he interacts with since they must always be cognizant of offending him. Less tolerant workplace associates are turned off by his excessively nice behavior, judging it as low-status attempts to ingratiate. This perplexes and aggravates the nice guy because in his view he was only being considerate, and so he may respond to any perceived rejection by becoming moody or standoffish, further alienating people.

The nice guy becomes ever more frustrated at his continued failure to get what he wants professionally, personally, and romantically, from friends, family, and potential love interests. This can result in the laying of guilt trips on others *("I was so considerate to you, yet you won't do the things I ask")*. This is a passive-aggressive manipulation tactic.

If anyone criticizes his behavior or points out that his expectations of people are unreasonable, the nice guy feels threatened and reacts with denial, defiance and anger. In extreme cases outbursts of violent rage may occur, which he justifies by projecting blame *(e.g., "it's your fault; you don't appreciate my kind, selfless efforts")*.

Again the victim part is played, complete with examples of how 'put upon' or 'mistreated' he feels. When done skillfully this can prompt feelings of guilt in others (along with fear of his recurring temper), but in the long run his anger and desire to control people (i.e., have them behave the way he wants) reveal him as the emotionally unstable guy who, deep down, puts his own interests first.

The man who exhibits these beliefs and behaviors may find it difficult to change, because of his refusal to take any responsibility for the consequences of his attitude and the conviction that other people make his life difficult, and those he was nice to now 'owe' him. The 'nice guy' blames (and punishes) others for his own shortcomings, failures and misery.

This self-defeating strategy can be practiced over many years or even an entire lifetime. It gets you nowhere, resulting in much unnecessary stress and conflict with others. Hopefully this does not resemble your situation, but if it does you need to take a long, honest look at yourself, and stop blaming everyone else for all your problems. Get rid of your rationalization that *the world is not fair to nice guys like me* and its associated victim mentality. Not only is it a false front, it serves nobody, least of all yourself.

Both Beliefs are Self-Deceptions

Your ego and the ways in which you manage and measure your self-worth can be your greatest ally or your worst enemy. If you feel inferior to everyone else, despair and anxiety will be your constant companions. If you hold to a moralistic superiority over your peers, bitterness and anger will eventually infect most of your relationships. Both conditions stand in the way of your happiness.

Additionally, people can detect these characteristics in others. Being reserved and depressed or resentful and demanding of people on a long-term basis is a social red flag, reducing their comfort level when engaging with you or even stopping them from seeking your company at all.

The reality is, you are neither inferior nor superior to those around you. Genetic diversity has insured that each of us possesses strengths and weaknesses. Chances are, the vast majority of your past failures (professional, personal, and romantic) can be traced to your negative perspective.

This genetic diversity has also produced optimists and pessimists. If after reading the book up to this point you are able to recognize some negative thought patterns in yourself, you should be commended because it is an important step towards self-improvement. However, if you refuse to believe that any predicament in which you find yourself is your own fault, you will likely continue to blame others for your failings and not make any progress.

Blaming Women

If you do not harbor anger and bitterness towards others for allegedly making your life difficult, you nevertheless may be understandably suspicious of any woman who says she wants to meet a good guy when so many of them seem to inexplicably pass you over for the so-called bad boys out there because they fail to see the dangerous part of the bad boy persona, mistaking it for confidence and strength rather than what it sometimes is – extreme risk.

Most women have trouble explaining what they want in a man, because there are so many subconscious factors at play. A woman may use logic and say she wants a nice guy but then her attention will be captured by all the assertive men she sees.

Some women make snap decisions. They like neat, exciting packages. This is an oversimplification, but it is true. If you stammer and fumble in the first few seconds of any interaction, she will form an opinion of you that will be hard to shake later.

Rather than dwell on this, it makes more sense to practice and polish your social skills so you don't make the same old mistakes to begin with. If you minimize your weaknesses and maximize your strengths, you will be far more attractive in any situation, from job interviews to dating.

Women may look upon men as being superficial for wanting to hook up with a blonde stick, as nice guys look upon women as superficial for wanting an assertive guy. These preferences are not necessarily superficial – to some degree they are evolutionary responses based on the attraction switches we are born with (though we all have individual preferences when it comes to who we find attractive).

It makes no sense to characterize women as a group as superficial or hard to please (so are job interviewers, of both sexes, for that matter), if for no other reason than this thought pattern will get you nowhere.

It would be nice if people made special allowances for you. It would be great if women threw themselves at you despite your reserved nature, or if a job interviewer gave you five chances to prove yourself instead of only one. But with so many other people to choose from, that is an unrealistic expectation. Why would they choose someone who is nervous when a more confident and relaxed applicant is just around the corner?

Sometimes all it takes to gain some of the qualities of an assertive bad boy is to engage in playful teasing of women, rather than always being overly agreeable. So you will need to modify your current behavior on the road to maximizing your potential.

Blaming outside factors for your shortcomings may give you some comfort, but it also gives you a reason to comfortably stay in your rut, doing nothing to improve your situation. But if you were to overhaul your core beliefs and gain some confidence (there are exercises for this in later sections), it will come across in your presentation, making you far more attractive.

Limiting Beliefs

The inferiority/superiority complexes cited above are examples of *misconceptions*. Similar to a misconception, a *Limiting Belief* is a negative conviction that becomes a self-fulfilling prophecy – that becomes a stark reality. For example, if you believe no woman would enjoy your approach, you are unlikely to ever confidently approach a woman.

In researching this book I spent some time on a shyness support group website to refresh my perspective on what it is like for extremely shy men and what they are doing to help their situation. I was struck with the number of members that were resigned to their lot in life, who believed they had an *unattractive personality* or who thought themselves to be so physically unattractive (self-described as "ugly") that no amount of positive attitude or personal grooming would help them.

Some referred to themselves as involuntarily celibate, or "incel" due to their perceived shortcomings, be they physical or psychological. Many of these guys were quite young, being in their teens to mid-twenties, with many believing the condition would be with them forever. I talked at length with a lot of men attending shyness support groups, and found that the older ones, about the age of 28 and up, had some hope for their future. Surprisingly, most of the younger ones would not listen to any argument to the contrary, which is ironic since the younger you are, the more years you have ahead of you to develop.

For example, many younger guys believed a man's attractiveness peaked at 25, diminishing rapidly thereafter, and held that any woman that was interested in an older man was only after his money. They refused to believe that gaining life experience and confidence had anything to do with attractiveness. Many men and women come of age in their thirties or even forties, enjoying a much richer social life than before, but some of the men in the support group absolutely refused to believe this fact.

Having had so little experience in life one wonders how a 21 year old can make such authoritative pronouncements on the nature of humankind and what the future holds. Some of them had not been on a single date in their life, but nonetheless thought they knew everything there was to know about women, i.e., they are all superficial bitches.

On the one hand, you can understand their bitterness, because they have the desire to be sociable and date, but feel powerless to enact those desires. This is an extremely frustrating condition, especially since if they could get a handle on their negativity some of these guys would have a lot to offer a woman if she could just see past his shyness. However, most were doing nothing to address their situation, preferring instead to give up and vent in an online forum.

Some people have not been blessed in the good looks department, but there are things you can do to maximize what you have, and minimize what you personally find unappealing. Have you ever run into a friend you haven't seen in years, who looked and acted so different you almost didn't recognize him? Some people who were formerly considered uninteresting or plain or unattractive take the initiative to transform themselves for the better. These people were dissatisfied with certain things about themselves and took steps to make positive changes.

Sometimes a new wardrobe, a better hairstyle, better posture can totally revamp your appearance. We'll get into style and personal grooming later on. They are the type of changes you can apply immediately and for immediate effect. Longer term, you can become more of a well-read person and increase your vocabulary (by becoming more familiar with current events, the arts, and adopting new hobbies) lose weight (or gain muscle mass if you consider yourself too thin) by eating more carefully and exercising regularly. A healthy body that is regularly exercised supports a healthy mind, clearer thinking, better sleep and the ability to make better decisions. Healthy, balanced eating and regular exercise do more for your confidence and self-esteem than you might imagine.

Other ways to change your appearance include experimenting with a beard (goatee, full beard, moustache, sideburns, or just the unshaven look), cutting your hair a different length than you normally do (the trend for the past 20 years has been shorter and shorter hair for men), wearing accessories (necklace or wrist band), wearing cool designer jeans that suit your body type instead of the old baggy ones you are used to, a sport jacket – the list goes on. Making a few of these changes can totally revamp your look. Clothes don't necessarily make the man, but they can help frame the sort of character and personality you can best project.

The psychological issues and confidence problems cannot be tackled overnight, but again, there are assignments in later chapters designed to help. The key to improvement is to approach my program with an open mind, and not give up when you experience setbacks.

Negative versus Positive Thoughts

As mentioned, an inferiority complex is almost a given with shy people. This can run from a fairly mild *I wish I was better at interacting with women* to *I can't interact well with anybody and I hate my life.* I'll assume you are somewhat closer to the latter.

Virtually every personality self-help book touts the virtues of having a positive self image, to which I agree wholeheartedly. But talk is cheap when you feel as if you are in a whirlpool of despair and can't swim out.

A little self-loathing isn't bad if it is constructive. Many famous, successful people have been hard on themselves, but they use it to drive themselves forward to succeed.

If left to run out of control negative thoughts can be paralyzing, leaving you to exist in despair. Overwhelming feelings that you are worthless or unskilled will keep you from accomplishing anything of merit in your lifetime, let alone allow you to date the woman of your dreams.

Self Recrimination

My worst habit has been dwelling on the past, kicking myself for what I thought were mistakes I made with women: failing to recognize when they were flirting with me, failing to have the courage to ask them out, or failing to understand when they just wanted to talk to me. Perhaps you are the same way. Dwelling on mistakes made days, weeks, or even years ago does absolutely no good – all it does is get you depressed.

You probably aren't depressed at work, because you are busy and interacting with others. You don't have the time to stew over what you think are your imperfections and inaction with women. However, if you spend your weekends at home alone with little to do, negative thoughts and depression are almost sure to come knocking.

There was a time in my life when I didn't look forward to weekends. So who doesn't like weekends? A guy that lets his social life so fall into ruin that he spends more time sulking than going out and doing things. After graduating from university I had such an abysmal social life I would actually be happier at work, even though I didn't particularly enjoy my job. This is a common problem if you spend a lot of time alone.

"When we are left alone, with no demands on attention, the basic disorder of the mind reveals itself. With nothing to do, it begins to follow random patterns, usually stopping to consider something painful or disturbing. Unless a person knows how to give order to his or her thoughts, attention will be attracted to whatever is most problematic in the moment; it will focus on some real or imagined pain, on recent grudges, or long-term frustrations. Entropy is the normal state of consciousness – a condition that is neither useful nor enjoyable."[3]

– Mihaly Csikszentmihalyi, Flow: The Psychology of Optimal Experience

In other words, the idle mind is seldom at peace; we dredge up all sorts of negative, worrisome subjects, dwell on our own mistakes in life and on perceived slights others have wrought upon us.

Talk about unproductive. Some of us spend as much time stewing in regret as we devote to surfing the internet and watching television. Imagine if you were to channel that time into bettering yourself, such as exploring a new hobby that gets you out of the house. The battle against your shyness would be over!

If your life is similar, moving on to a different, more sociable routine will allow you to get down to the business of making your life better. But even so, the ability to "give order to his or her thoughts" is invaluable in avoiding such periods of despair. Learning meditative and relaxation techniques will be of value here, as is developing the ability to recognize and avoid negative emotions as they creep in will greatly diminish their influence over you.

I recommend you make several changes in your life: a new wardrobe, wearing accessories, going out for walks and interacting with people, engaging in behavior that takes you out of your comfort zone (such as signing up for special interest evening courses), and more. They all work in concert to help you mentally. There is a cumulative effect, one that increases as you transition into owning the changes you've made.

You probably won't notice any difference in your social life if all you do is change your wardrobe and go out one night a month. Likewise, banishing most negative thoughts may reduce your depression, but it won't get you a date if you don't engage with people or have poor personal hygiene. You must commit to making changes and improvements in *all aspects of your life* in order to reach and maintain your goal.

Making many small, sequential changes, and committing to them will help you achieve a strong, positive state of mind, a necessary condition for improving your interaction with others. The changes I advocate for you will not involve putting up a front of confidence, but will help you develop the real thing.

Change from a Pessimist to an Optimist

Nobody likes to admit these negative personality traits in themselves. Sure, you admit you're shy because it is an obvious, debilitating problem, but are you able to admit other, slightly less obvious aspects that are also working against you?

Social Anxiety Disorder is sometimes accompanied with rationalizations or exaggerated doom and gloom explanations, such as *people are cruel, that's why I have difficulty with others*. Yes, some people can be cruel, but most aren't. If someone doesn't go out of their way to be nice to you, or make special allowances for your shyness, that doesn't mean they are evil. But some people seem to thrive on negativity. They:

- Look for the worst in every situation
- Constantly complain about things (including other people)
- Fixate on their flaws, downplaying their positive attributes
- Make up excuses for their own failures (blaming other people or society)
- Make up excuses for not challenging themselves (thinking they will only be disappointed)
- Are often in a gloomy mood
- Rarely complimenting anyone

If your own outlook matches more than a couple of these characteristics, you have some work to do, in particular because people don't like to hang around others that are constantly depressed or complaining about how awful the world is. If you inflict these moods on others it has surely had an effect; they may not seek out your company as often as they otherwise would, or worse, stop hanging around with you entirely.

Watch for these negative traits in yourself in the future. Catch yourself before you utter a negative comment. And instead of being silent as the only alternative, find something positive to say, preferably about the person you are talking to.

Second, don't sit there being in a bad mood, fixating on how everyone and everything is terrible. Everyone isn't terrible. They're just trying to get through life, like you. So keep this in mind whenever negative thoughts creep in.

Third, you must be positive about all the changes you are going to make in order to start enjoying your life. Instead of dwelling on how much time it will take or how difficult it will be, think about how you will notice small, cumulative positive changes that will add up, allowing you to enjoy your life like never before.

Reframing

You can reframe any negative situation into a positive one, in effect, put a positive spin on your future. For example, instead of dwelling on how awkward you are in social situations, think about how you are improving yourself already by the simple act of picking up and reading this book. It shows you are looking to improve your situation by enacting its suggestions and exercises.

Most shy people are very hard on themselves. They are their own worst critics. You may have one or more of these phrases as these to describe yourself or your failures:

- I'm an idiot
- I make stupid decisions
- I'm always going to be shy and awkward

We all feel bad when we make a mistake (social or otherwise), but talk like that is counterproductive. Imagine speaking to a friend or relative that way after they made an unintentional error. It would be absolutely unacceptable to treat someone in that manner, and would do nothing to improve the situation.

Some self-criticism is healthy if it prompts you to forge ahead in your efforts, but if you truly hate yourself you are more likely to sit idle in a pool of despair. Don't be like some of the guys on the shyness support sites, who have given up, and channel all their energy into complaining about their lives rather than taking positive action.

Self-loathing can be detected by others. It comes across in your body language, how you react to difficulties or criticism, your facial expression, the way you dress and more. It is one more characteristic that stands in your way.

A very astute woman once said to me, *"If you don't love yourself, how do you expect others to love you?"*

If you catch yourself making a mistake, it is far more productive to give positive reinforcement:

- I made a mistake (or social goof); I will learn from the experience so it is unlikely to happen again
- I'm not going to waste time regretting past errors, I'm going to look forward to the future and better my social skills

In any negative situation, if you reframe it using positive instead of negative language, it helps keep you from descending into a morose and negative state of mind. This will be a powerful tool in reshaping your overall outlook to one of optimism.

Everyone has to start somewhere, and very few people are naturals out of the gate. If your dating life thus far has been disappointing, think of it this way: from this moment onward you are addressing that problem and working towards a solution.

The public is not out to judge you

A negative thought pattern reinforces your present belief that your every move is being critiqued, with people taking note of what you think is your funny walk, your stiff movements, your weak voice, your crummy clothes, your feeble attempts at communication.

If you are completely self-conscious about all these self-professed faults, then yes, people will notice. If you are at a gathering attempting to take a sip of your tea, but think *oh no, everyone is staring at me, thinking what a loser I am,* you are probably going to smack your tooth with the cup, spill your tea, lose your balance and fall into the shrimp platter. That would definitely call attention to yourself. So your fear became a self-fulfilling prophecy. Had you been a little more relaxed, nobody would have given you a second glance (except perhaps to admire the nice jacket you're wearing – the one I suggest later in the book).

People are far too preoccupied with their lives to dwell on the little quirks of others. So this fear of being examined for your flaws is unfounded. What they notice is your low self-esteem. The fact that you are self-conscious draws negative attention.

Again, a big part of getting out of the low self esteem gutter is to stop thinking of others as superior. You may think that other people have gotten all aspects of their lives together, have lots of friends and few fears. Some people have all those attributes, but most do not. Some insecure people still act like children, covering up their fears by ridiculing others, or by putting up a front of confidence (e.g., bragging about their car, high-paying job, etc.) when they are in reality very insecure.

People who have great lives generally don't go around bragging or ridiculing others; they tend to be non-judgmental.

Two

BE PROACTIVE:
CHART a NEW DIRECTION

Some people believe nobody can change; that is, once you are born with a certain personality, it is locked into you for good. This is only partly true – I'm not going to get into the "nature versus nurture" debate, but behaviors and reactions to situations can be molded. Take soldiers for instance. Many new recruits are rebellious, unfocused eighteen year olds, but send them off to basic training for ten weeks and they become disciplined men able to engage in battle when ordered.

This doesn't mean you must be young in order to improve yourself. I know of many people that completely changed their careers into their forties, going back to college in an entirely new direction, learning new skills.

In this program you won't be exposed to a drill sergeant forcing you to do push-ups if you screw up, but if you want it badly enough you can improve yourself. It requires four things: a *plan, motivation, effort,* and *time*.

Before you get discouraged at the "time" part, know this: the more motivation you possess and the more effort you put in, the less time it will take for you to improve your situation.

As for the **Plan**, that is where this book comes in. The tips, advice, and assignments target all three degrees of shyness. Some can be applied immediately; others require some preparation to implement.

The **Motivation** is obvious; you long to improve your social life, with women in particular. This might even be your number one desire, ahead of finding a satisfying career.

The **Effort** must come from you and you alone. This book can act as a guide and coach, but you must be willing to put in the effort to complete (and repeat) the assignments. If you read the book once and only put in a token effort, you won't make progress.

As for the **Time** . . . we're all used to the quick fix. Fast food takes the time and effort out of cooking. High-speed internet cuts the download time for that new media file. But conditioning yourself to a new behavior may require more effort than you are used to. Remember that it took you all of your life so far to become what you are right now and to feel the way you feel right now, so repairing, adjusting and improving all of that will take more than a few days. The effects of years cannot be undone by thinking a few rosy thoughts. Time will be your friend here.

Take weight training for example (this is something I recommend later in the book, as one way to improve your self-esteem). If you are out of shape and hit the gym in an effort to gain some muscle, you won't notice much difference during the first few weeks. But as sure as the next full moon, you will inexorably improve, gaining muscle mass. Persistent regular exercise pays off over time – for your entire life. Again, time is your friend.

Think of how many people join a gym in early January to fulfill their new year's resolution to lose weight. Most quit after a couple of weeks, upset that they did not lose any weight for what they view as a monumental effort. For those few that stick with it, they lose weight, gain muscle and cardiovascular fitness, and transform themselves. And once they have reached a certain level, it gets easier to maintain their fitness, and they start to enjoy the formerly painful experience of going to the gym. Start slowly, gain strength and confidence, then increase the scope of your regular exercise until you reach the level needed to maintain a physical condition with which you're happy and confident.

How badly do you want it? How much time and effort are you willing to put in, so you can realize a better quality of life?

Some people need a lot of repetition in order to change their behavior. I was one of those people, at least when it came to interacting with women. Keep this book handy, re-read, repeat, and follow its guidelines.

The theories are simple to understand, but putting them into practice requires dedication and patience. My success can translate into your success, because this book contains the benefits of the real-life experiences of someone who has been there.

Some of the changes I suggest might feel foreign. I'm not advocating that you turn your personality inside out in some misguided effort to become a class clown. But if you start with minor changes you will eventually work towards a lifestyle that will bring welcome transformations to your social life.

Do Not be Resistant to Change

It is human nature to be resistant to change, especially if up until now you have had a pessimistic outlook on life. It is important to eliminate any limiting beliefs – self-limiting and widely touted statements like *nobody can change* and *once you hit 30 your personality and habits are set for life* and other nonsense. They're all unsupportable and negatively self-serving myths that limit your ability to evolve as a person.

Will the changes be real, and accepted by others?

If I change my attitude, wardrobe, and other things in my life, my family and friends who have known me for years won't buy it and won't accept the new me. They'll think I'm faking it or will tell me to stop this nonsense.

That argument doesn't hold water. In 90% of cases people accept changes in others without negative comments.

All of us have seen a major change in others, and (provided it is a positive change) we accept the new reality, usually without a second thought. Think of the kid that is picked on by the school bully over the entire school year. Everyone looks upon him as weak, and resigned to his fate. Then one day he stands up to the bully, giving him a black eye or scaring him off or simply outstaring him. The kid isn't bullied anymore. The other kids accept this as the new truth.

There used to be a short, overweight guy at a company where I worked. He had a reputation as being the jolly fat guy who was always smiling and laughing. But he seemed to have an undercurrent of resentment, as if he didn't like being thought of by the rest of the staff in that way. Then over several months he transformed himself. He became slim and trim, and a little more serious. Though he was always competent at his job, he became more driven and focused as he lost weight, changing many things about himself at the same time.

Eventually he lost the jolly fat guy image entirely. In fact, he started offering introductory boxing courses to fellow employees after work. I've never seen a more complete makeover in a person, and not a single staff member made a disparaging remark during or after the process. Everyone accepted the new reality without question.

While negative comments are rare, unfortunately there is a greater chance you will hear them from a close friend or family member, who due to their familiarity tend to possess a sense of behavioral entitlement when it comes to making their opinion known, sometimes through disparaging remarks. If it is not an occasional good-natured ribbing – that is, if it takes on a repeated, condescending tone – it is likely the person has control issues or at the very least just doesn't know how the comments can be counterproductive and even hurtful. Persistent exposure to such negativity can impact your frame of mind and your progress, so make it clear to the person that their comments are not helpful.

It will take too long to change myself (or I'm too old to change), so why bother?

No matter your age, if you are constantly experiencing feelings of regret at how many years you wasted in not taking action, you may still think changing your lifestyle will take too long. This is another prime example of a limiting belief, one that helps keep the extremely reserved person locked in their cage. Ask yourself this question: *How long will I continue to practice habits and attitudes that haven't done me much good so far?* If something isn't working for you, it's definitely time to replace it with something else.

At every age there are people making life changing decisions – in midlife, going back to school in their thirties or forties, getting a new university degree to increase their chances of advancement in their chosen field, or simply jumping at the opportunity to start over with something new. I used to take martial arts, and some of the students going for their belt tests (including some going for their black belt) were over forty, a few of them in their fifties.

The thought of taking months or years to achieve your goal can be daunting, but think of it this way. Life is a process, filled with transformations. We change jobs, relationships, even friendships. Without change, your life stagnates and doesn't advance. Many of these changes take time, yet we go through them without a second thought. Embracing and planning for change can be an important factor in overcoming shyness and lack of confidence. Life is full of possibilities:

- **It has always been a dream of yours to visit Africa and see the Savannah. It might take you a couple of years of saving your money before you'll be able to afford it. Does that mean you won't bother?**
- **Your boss likes your work and wants you to oversee a new division. It will mean a big pay raise, but it will require a few months of night school to acquire the training. Are you going to refuse, and stay at a lower pay level?**
- **You have always dreamed of being an artist or performer or song writer, but developing this hobby to its potential may take years. Does that mean you will ignore your dream, and spend your free time watching television instead?**

It generally takes a few years to get good at something, but you can shorten this time through dedication. Journalist and pop economics author Malcolm Gladwell in his book *Outliers: The Story of Success* suggests that 10,000 hours of practice (which amounts to 20 hours of work per week for 10 years in case you were wondering) is required to become the very best at something. Don't be discouraged, because we're not talking here about becoming the best in the world at something – we're talking about getting *good at something*. That's much more manageable, achievable and useful and it doesn't require anywhere near 10,000 hours.

For instance, think of any new sport you have taken up, and are now proficient at (something you practiced regularly, not just dabbled in occasionally). Returning to the martial arts example, if you show a good degree of dedication, you can get your black belt in two or three years of study, however I've seen some people who were extremely focused get it in about a year. Attractive, no doubt, but we all work at new things at a pace we can manage. The point is to persistently embrace the effort in order to achieve some degree of success or to adapt to changes.

The same goes for other sports. If you go out skiing every weekend in the winter you can go from being a beginner to expert in as little as two years. I witnessed this first-hand with several people. But if you only go out two or three times a year, you won't progress much at all. I know someone who has skied for over twenty years, but has never taken a lesson and rarely makes it out to the hill. As a result he is no better than an intermediate.

You can progress similarly when it comes to social aptitude. While taking a series of improv courses, I saw several individuals go from being nervous, hesitant beginners to excellent performers who shed their stage fright in only a few months.

The process of improving your social life will take some time. In fact, to fully realize your potential you will need to adopt new hobbies, interests, skills, and attitudes, much like the examples above, and practice on a consistent basis.

I've been lonely, miserable and in this rut for as long as I can remember. How can I expect the future to be different?

This way of thinking is common. After all, if you have been in the same dreary routine for a long time, it can be difficult to imagine living any other way. But you will need to shake off that attitude quickly, otherwise your own negative thoughts will sabotage your progress before you even get started.

The jolly fat guy example is relevant here again. The man was overweight (and, in his own view, unattractive) for years, but had grown tired of that existence. Do you think it was easy for him to transform into a trim, athletic go-getter? Yet he did it in under a year. Patient persistence paid off. He wouldn't have been able to make those major changes in his life if he had viewed his goal to be too difficult or time consuming. He formed a plan of action, but then concentrated only on achieving each incremental step. Nobody can look at some large plan and not feel uncertainty at some point. But break that same plan into more manageable chunks and everything in it becomes achievable.

By gradually adopting and practicing a series of new habits aimed at developing a more sociable existence you will improve your life. When negative thoughts or fears creep in, it is your duty to kick them aside and look to the future. Your future is whatever you want it to be. Don't let anyone tell you otherwise.

Should I let my family and friends in on my plan?

It is your choice whether to inform others of this journey of self-improvement. Personally, I would avoid making any grand announcements and just get the job done. However, if you have a friend or someone you met online that is in the same situation, you might want to be each other's coach, helping each other through each milestone.

Or, seek out someone with a good social life for advice. A mentor that you trust can be an invaluable asset to your development, helping and encouraging you through the process.

A Metaphor for Life

From early adulthood we all embark on a journey to find a mate. All of us must go through this voyage, some finding it more difficult than others. You may have many false starts and setbacks along the way. Some people seem to have better luck than most or appear to be naturals. The majority experience multiple difficulties, but are able to learn from their mistakes, and so can make progress fairly quickly.

The unfortunate few make the same mistakes over and over, and have trouble progressing. These individuals must learn to make changes in how they deal with failure. When a setback is encountered it is tempting to give in to depression and quit. This is a no-win scenario. The key is to admit a negative attitude and realize that an unchanging, unsuccessful strategy is self-defeating. When stuck in an ineffective routine you must be willing to make major changes in order to succeed.

Imagine for a moment that it is customary each year for hundreds of men to sail away from their coastal village in search of a wife. Each man travels solo in his smallish one-person sailboat, crossing thousands of miles of ocean to the next continent, where single women await.

No two voyagers have the same experience. Some are able to navigate through most storms unscathed, while others suffer damage to their vessel, forcing a stop at an island for repairs before continuing. Once repaired, further storms may be encountered, forcing yet another detour.

Some of these individuals give up and remain alone on the island, thinking it is too difficult to continue. Others persevere, not giving up despite bad luck and multiple setbacks.

Some make the journey without much contact with fellow sailors; others meet up for a while to share stories and advise each other. Some are hostile, attempting to sabotage anyone they encounter. Soon word spreads among the loosely-bound group of voyagers about who among them are cooperative, and who are to be avoided.

During good weather, some sailors tend to their boat and make sure everything is in good working order, performing regular maintenance. Others just sit on deck enjoying the sun, not noticing frayed rope, torn sails, or rotten wood. Some of these neglectful sailors pay the price for being lazy when their sail tears away or their mast collapses, forcing a stop. Of these, some curse their luck, believing the whole ordeal is unfair, and continue to ignore needed maintenance, and the cycle repeats itself. Others realize their own inaction was the cause of the setback and change their routine, looking for weak areas that need attention, thus helping to avoid future disaster.

The diligent sailors (especially the cooperative ones) are better able to weather any further storms; they've learned from their (and other's) experiences and avoid past mistakes. They take note of what works and what doesn't, and can thus increase their rate of progress.

The most adaptable sailors are able to make the crossing in a few months. Some take many years or don't make it at all, believing the world is against them and the task is impossible, so they remain on their island, alone. The rest are able to make the journey in one or two years, because (despite setbacks) they believed in themselves and were able to *adapt* and apply lessons learned along the way.

For some of us, entering the dating world is no easier than crossing the ocean. Yet people do it. It is a test of will and many experience discouraging setbacks along the way. During difficult times many of these adventuresome souls probably wish they could turn back for the safety of their home, but most do not, despite the hardship. And once completed, none of them regret embarking on the journey, looking back on it as a defining time of their life.

Lifestyle Choices that Lead to Misery

Most of us practice bad habits without even realizing it that make us unhappy. Living your life in an endless, unchanging pattern of waking up, going to work, coming home to watch television, surf the web or hit a social network site, then going to bed is an easy routine to get into, and a sure way to depression.

Addictions

You may have latched onto some unhealthy habits like smoking, drinking excessively, wasting endless hours online, or doing drugs. Quitting an addiction is not an easy process, requiring discipline and sometimes outside help.

Addictions of any kind will hinder your social progress. And since many of the exercises in this book require you to get out of your comfort zone, be aware that if you do have a debilitating addiction you will need to address it before going any further. Seek out a support group or therapist that specializes in the area of concern.

Mundane Routines

If you work full time and are tired at the end of the day, you may think you simply don't have the energy to do anything besides mindless surfing when you get home. You may be tired, but the human body has amazing capacity to rise to an occasion when called upon, so you will be able to devote one or two week nights to a new hobby or skill.

Eating Habits

If you eat poorly you will always feel run down. Soft drinks, pizza, french fries, other fried foods, excess salt, too few vegetables and fruits on a daily basis and too much bread and baking not only sap your energy but can also lead to physical health problems. Improving your eating habits goes hand in hand with exercise. Laying off the fries and sugared soft drinks will make it easier to keep weight off. And it doesn't need to be painful – if you are a fast food addict you can still get the burger, but instead of the soft drink and fries, get it with salad, low-fat dressing and bottled water.

Emerging from your Seclusion, one step at a time

But first things first. If you describe your condition as paralyzing, you can use the internet to your advantage, and start conditioning yourself to a higher level of social interaction than you are used to. Assuming you don't have much of an online presence, you could engage in several on-line enthusiast forums.

Concentrating your efforts on Facebook or similar sites is usually counterproductive. Most Facebook friends are not real friends. Some people build up their friend count as a matter of status. I'll give you an example; my Facebook page states I took a course in Public Relations. One guy I had never seen before sent me a message asking if he could buy my textbook, since he was taking the course the following year. I declined his offer because even though I was no longer in school I liked the book and wanted to keep it. We had only communicated once via email, for this one issue. I never expected to hear from him again. Yet, weeks later, he attempted to add me to his friends list. I declined.

I wasn't trying to be rude. It's just that I would expect to have some sort of at least occasional interaction with someone (even if it is just on-line) before I add (or am added) to a friend list. I suppose that's why some people have hundreds, if not thousands, of friends, most of whom they will never even correspond with, let alone meet in person. For most people the criteria for being on a friends list are almost non-existent.

That is why I advocate an active internet presence beyond posting on your Facebook wall or Google+ circle what you had for breakfast this morning. For instance, if you have an interest in video games, cycling, music, model airplane building or any other hobby, join some enthusiast sites and start posting questions or describe your progress.

Enthusiast sites cater to specialized interests and offer interactions of far more depth than any of the general social networking sites. If you are knowledgeable in any area you may soon find yourself giving more advice than you are asking. There is a good chance you will develop online friendships, some of which may translate to in-person friendships. At the very least, developing your ability to equitably, calmly and patiently seek and offer facts, details, opinions and advice about your particular interest will help you become a better communicator.

Additionally, there are online social support groups out there that address fears such as public speaking and shyness in general. These can offer a positive experience, but beware that there are some terminally negative people who are all doom and gloom about their prospects, citing things such as their looks and what they term the superficial nature of women that create insurmountable boundaries to ever finding love.

It makes you wonder why such people remain on the forums and message boards, since they see no prospects and only want to vent and have people feel sorry for them. By all means try and cheer them up, but should your words not have any effect, move on before they drag you down with them. They're lonely and miserable and you can't fix them. The old saying that misery loves company is absolutely true. Instead, concentrate on participating with people who are open to actually improving their life.

Another idea is to become an online reviewer of consumer products (where you can write movie, gaming or product reviews). Many sites exist for this (Epinions, for one), on every conceivable topic and product. Your reviews may prompt questions and comments from readers, which allow you to engage with them and offer advice.

If you post a question or an experience on an enthusiast forum and don't get a reply, don't be discouraged. It could be that nobody had an answer for your particular question, or the question had been asked many times before and is present in the *Frequently Asked Questions* (FAQ) section of the site. Most message boards and forums have decent search tools. You can type a simple search phrase and quickly find all current and previous discussions about a particular item, subject or topic. Do that search before you ask questions. On many sites, asking a question which turns out to have been asked and answered many times before is a really good way to inadvertently ostracize yourself. In most cases, joining a site may involve a small period of acclimatization until you are comfortable. Lurk in the forums and message boards for a couple of weeks after joining a site to get the feel of the place.

Some posters like to trash talk and ridicule everyone who doesn't agree with their positions. They're usually referred to online as trolls. Don't take them or their comments personally, or better yet, ignore them entirely and instead add your own posts to discussion threads in which sincere and positive people are participating. Be the mature one, the sage giver of fair advice for the newbies. The trolls are probably even shyer than you, with one key difference – they haven't taken the initiative to better themselves, as you have. The calm, knowledgeable persona that you develop online will be a great template for refining your face-to-face personality.

Some online posters are very prolific, and gain an online following. Most have the following traits in common:

- **They make an honest effort to post useful information that will help others**
- **Their posts are friendly and accessible, without being condescending**
- **They are generous, pointing readers to other areas for additional information**
- **They avoid arguments by keeping disagreements on a courteous level**
- **When strong disagreements take place, they disengage after expressing their opinion clearly and supportably; they realize that they don't need to win the disagreement**

By comporting themselves thus, these people gain a lot of respect in their online community.

As you post in the forums and write reviews, work on your writing skills and gradually increase the length and depth of your reviews. Avoid writing as if you are texting someone; e.g., don't use "ur" as a substitute for *your* and *you are*. Everyone, especially women, appreciates a person who can string a proper sentence together.

If your writing skills need some polish, enroll in an online writing course, offered by local community colleges. Better yet, attend one in person (getting out and attending courses is important and is discussed below).

If you only join one online forum and make one post every two weeks, you will not make much progress. The goal is to become prolific (a 'star contributor'), and to establish yourself as a valued member of the online community. Make several posts a day on multiple topics. Make it so other readers eventually look forward to reading what you have to say.

Assignment #1:
Online Contributions

Set the following goals for online forums:

- **Join three distinct online communities (not just three separate online forums in the same field).**
- **Make several posts per week in each community, with the ultimate goal of gaining knowledge and helping others.**

The best special interest forums are usually the ones with strong, fair Moderators. Look for such forums covering your particular area of interest – photography, gaming, skiing, sports of all kinds, auto repair, model making, woodworking, personal financial management, etc., etc. – the list is almost endless. Set the following goals for online review sites:

- **Review as many products as possible (products that you own or returned, movies you've seen, music you've purchased, services you've used)**
- **Make constructive comments on other people's reviews, even if it is a simple "Congratulations on a well-written review."**

Remember you're practicing new techniques for self-improvement, not finding excuses to get online and remain there. Limit your online commitment to one hour per day, three or four times per week..

With your progress in other social areas with people (e.g., face to face interaction) your online interactions will naturally wane, because you will have been too busy with friends or a girlfriend – good times indeed. As you begin to master the online world, it is time to venture forth.

Working on your Voice

Use a digital recorder and speak some lines from a book. Also record your side of a phone conversation. Do you speak clearly or mumble? Do you start off at a decent volume, but then trail sentences off until you are inaudible? Do you speak too quickly? Are you afraid of pauses, trying to fill every second of time with chatter? Does the end of many of your answers to simple questions use a rising tone that sounds almost like a question itself?

Actors are trained to enunciate words so they are clearly understood. You can do the same by adjusting your volume, paying attention to pronunciation (ensuring each word is said clearly, so they don't blur together), slowing down your speech if necessary, and allowing pauses where warranted.

During conversations, before speaking, take a deep breath. This serves two purposes. First, it fills your lungs with air, so that you can talk without searching for your breath if you are nervous. Secondly, it relaxes you. Don't worry about the slight pause in conversation as you inhale; if anything, it can make you appear to be a thoughtful speaker.

If you are nervous you may sometimes either speak faster than necessary or become tongue-tied and unable to utter more than a few quiet words. This first has the effect of making your voice sound higher-pitched, and it betrays your nervousness. The second has the effect of making people strain to understand or hear you. Both make you appear weak (or submissive). By taking a breath before speaking, you give yourself a chance to assemble your thoughts, moderate your pitch and speed, and appear in control.

Practice this a few times, then record yourself again. Do not be afraid to pause to gather your thoughts! You will be amazed at the change.

Telephone conversations

How do you come across to others on the phone? There are many people that have very poor telephone manners. They answer lazily or gruffly, they speak in monosyllables, and are generally impolite (or just lazy).

When answering a call, don't grunt into the mouthpiece. Say "Hello" clearly and in an upbeat manner (in other words, don't bark the word out as if the person is disturbing you). When conversing, be polite. If you made the phone call and need to speak with someone other than the person that picked up the phone, say "May I please speak with Don?" rather than just "is Don there?" The former has a lot more class and will usually elicit a courteous response.

I'm even polite to telemarketers. They usually start the conversation by asking how I am. I always reply with "Fine, how are you?" This never fails to take them off guard; I've had several say that nobody ever asks them how they are.

I usually let them speak just long enough so I know what they are selling, just in case I am interested, but if I am not interested in their product I never let them go through their entire sales pitch (which can otherwise take several minutes). I politely interrupt by saying, "Pardon me, but I'm really not interested, and I don't want you to waste time on your sales pitch when you could be going on to the next person that might be interested. But thanks anyway." If they persist, I thank them again and hang up.

Besides getting a crank call, this is the only situation where it is acceptable to hang up on a person, because simply saying "no thanks" to a telemarketer is usually not enough to end the call normally.

For other phone conversations, if you are nervous, there are a few things you can practice to eliminate the nerves.

Do banking transactions or credit card payments by phone rather than internet. You will no doubt be prompted to enter keypad numbers in order to identify your account, but in the end specify you wish to speak to a real person for the transaction. The banking representatives are usually courteous and professional, with a clear way of speaking that you can emulate in your own conversations. If you doubt your confidence altogether, prior to making the phone call write down a list of questions or a list of information you wish to obtain. A list is one of the best ways to eliminate situations in which nervousness causes you to forget important things. Some of the brightest most apparently confident men in the world use short lists to help keep themselves on track in discussions, interviews, phone calls, meetings, seminars and other situations.

Call local colleges and ask them for information on business presentation courses and public speaking courses. Try and speak with the course coordinator or teacher, and in advance have some questions written down that you can ask, before requesting that they send some information to you (this exercise, if you haven't already guessed by now, also has the practical aspect of letting you know what courses exist for actually enrolling in the course).

Call relatives to see how they are doing (especially ailing relatives – they will be very glad to hear a friendly voice, and it will be good to strengthen your bonds with family). Stay upbeat, focus on the positive. Re-establish contact with old friends – ask how they are doing, reminisce about old times, ask about their future plans. Prepare your list of questions for them and your list of information about yourself in advance.

For really advanced telephone exercises, volunteer your time for the local chapter of your school alumni fundraising group, a local politician who is trying to win the next election, or an environmental or charitable organization that you support. All of these will have calling scripts for you to follow, so you will not have to wing it on the phone. As you get more comfortable on the phone you will develop an easier conversational style, so it will sound less like you are reading from a script.

This last bit is advanced stuff – you will now be a telemarketer! But don't let that scare you off, since it is volunteer work for a cause. If you join such a group that needs people to call for donations, etc., some people you call will be hostile. Don't take it personally – it is not you they are angry at, but the organization that has a policy to call people at home. This will be great training in dealing with people. There is a script for this too (remain calm, thank them for their time, and say good bye). Organizations will be extremely grateful for any phone volunteering you can do, and will bend over backwards to answer any concerns you have.

You must do these exercises repeatedly for there to be any progress. The side benefit is that you will have a better connection with your relatives and friends. Plus once you become more comfortable you will be a more marketable employment prospect.

Lists and practice will also help you when talking to women over the phone, such as those you may have met on an online dating site. But to truly sound good over the phone, you must compensate for the telephone's inherent shortcomings. Since the person can't see you, they won't know if you are smiling, gesturing, winking, or doing any other unconscious physical embellishment to your speaking voice. People are visual creatures, so when they only hear your voice, there is a missing component that keeps them from seeing the complete you.

If you have a dry wit style of humor it may not come across as intended over the phone, as it requires the listener to interpret subtle nuance or inflection in your tone of voice. In other words, they don't 'get' sarcasm or irony unless they have visual clues as well. Never joke sarcastically or ironically with any woman without first figuring out if they'll understand what you're trying to do. A lot of people need to simultaneously hear your vocal inflections and see your facial expressions in order to laugh along with you at some funny sarcasm or ironic comment.

It's unavoidable – phone conversations are less energetic than in-person conversations. With practice you can make up for this. If the person says something funny, don't just smile, but let out a real laugh.

Here's a real life example of the perils of poor phone presentation. A woman I met online called me, and we were having a good time, or so I thought. She was funny and clever, and I thought I was matching her banter and wit. But after a few minutes, she asked me why I was so serious. I was taken by surprise because I was enjoying the conversation so much I was smiling almost constantly. Then I realized all she could hear was my voice, and my tendency to speak without much inflection made it seem as if I wasn't really having a good time.

I resolved from then on to be more energetic. Through many phone conversations since that incident, a woman has never again had occasion to ask me that question, and I've have had a better success rate of phone conversations leading to an actual date.

Case Study – A Telephone Sales Job

After my involvement in the university guidebook, my success led to a job as the student newspaper's advertising salesperson. Though useful in helping my telephone confidence, the guidebook had been a short-term gig. The newspaper was for the entire school year, with a much deeper client list, and since I was still very reserved it was a trial by fire.

Being so far out of my comfort zone was frightening, and yet I saw the potential to gain some real-world job experience, set my own hours, and possibly make some decent money. These motivating factors allowed me to quickly shift from being an insecure caller to a confident business professional. I did this by:

- Having a calling script to get me through the initial part of the conversation
- Believing that I was providing a valued service to the customer, which came across in my presentation
- Not letting an initial "no thanks" answer discourage me from calling the next business

The result was a sales record for the year, money in my pocket, and after just a couple of weeks of solid practice talking on the phone for a minimum of two hours per day, or about fifteen potential clients per day, I had obliterated my fear of talking on the phone.

Assignment #2:
Voice & Telephone Clarity

- Record your voice and work on any clarity issues (most can be addressed by simply slowing down your speaking, and taking a deep breath before starting).
- Make calls to relatives, telephone banking, and community colleges (to inquire about presentation courses).
- Volunteer to man the phone for charity, political candidate, or alumni. Better yet, get a telemarketing job (you don't need to do this forever, but even a few weeks in such a job will transform your telephone skills for the better).

Personal Grooming

Make no mistake. Having a good personality wins women over. This includes being relaxed, spontaneous, humorous and assertive. But what opens the door is style. Working on your inner self is an ongoing process that is addressed throughout this book, but in this section we will address your outer self.

Take an honest look at your appearance. This may seem obvious, but lots of guys look sloppy. Do you shower every day? Have greasy hair? Dandruff? Stains on your shirt? Do you need to trim your nasal or eyebrow hair? Do you bother wearing underarm deodorant? Or do you go overboard, splashing on the cheap cologne, giving everyone on the bus an allergy attack?

I'm assuming you brush your teeth at least every morning and evening, but do you floss every night before going to bed? If you don't you should. Flossing is the single best thing you can do to avoid bad breath. If you never floss, a small shred of last Wednesday's steak may still be residing between your back molars, missed by your toothbrush, decaying and creating a foul smell that may be undetectable to you, but is very apparent to anyone you are speaking to.

Or you may have short-term bad breath from that Caesar salad you had for lunch. Always carry some breath mints for after meals.

Tasteful cologne is usually appreciated by women. Try a few samples in a reputable store. If your workplace has a no-scent policy you may have to confine your cologne wearing to the weekends, but you may be allowed to wear a lightly-scented deodorant. I prefer deodorant to antiperspirant, which contains aluminum compounds that clog your pores, preventing sweat and eventually results in build-up of product residue on your shirts (that can remain even after washing).

If you have any nasty workplace habits such as clipping your fingernails at your desk or in the lunch room, chewing with your mouth open, spitting in the lunch room sink, or blowing your nose into the washroom basin (e.g., by pressing one nostril and exhaling forcefully in the general direction of the washroom sink), end those practices immediately. Don't laugh – I have witnessed all of this, and more, from some employees at a Fortune 500 company in a major city.

Develop some Style

Are most of your clothes over two years old? Do they fit properly? Are the colors starting to fade? Do you consistently under-dress in order to feel 'comfortable?' If your clothes are old and drab, that's one more reason for women to pass you by. Time for a new wardrobe. Go shopping. Find a store (or two, or three) that sells decent clothing with well-trained staff that can help find some good looks for you.

Certain body types look better with specific clothing patterns and styles. If you're short and stocky, or tall but self-conscious about how skinny you are, a knowledgeable sales clerk can steer you in the right direction about what looks best on you.

Don't be afraid to class up a bit. If you dress just slightly better than your co-workers (but not your boss) you will be sending a subtle message that you care about how you present yourself to your company. This also works on the street – when I took to wearing sport jackets during spring and fall while walking outside I noticed an increase in favorable glances from women.

This is something you should do on a consistent basis. Don't just buy one good shirt to wear on Mondays. Upgrade your entire wardrobe (if money is tight look for sales, and rearrange your budget to include a modest clothes buying trip every month). As you buy new clothes, give your old stuff to charity so it is not taking up space in your closet, tempting you to wear it again.

Don't confine your nice clothes to work. If you are going food shopping, forget those old jeans – wear designer jeans, or khakis, and your jacket. If it's too hot out, get some nice dress polo shirts or cool button-up short sleeved – and never tuck your shirt into your pants without a jacket (however, these days you can even keep your shirt untucked with a jacket). And wear a nice belt (even if it won't always be seen).

Don't forget to wear nice shoes – women notice. In fact, a date told me she was glad I didn't wear running shoes with my sport jacket, which is apparently a common mistake. Walking shoes can be comfortable to wear every day and yet be stylish enough to let you easily pass a club's dress code. Buying one pair in black and another in brown covers almost your entire wardrobe. Keep them clean.

White socks are out; your socks should be the same color as your shoes or pants. If during warm weather you are wearing deck shoes or sandals, ditch the socks altogether (whether you are wearing pants or shorts).

The same goes for undershirts – white is not fashionable. Buy several t-shirts of different colors to match your outerwear.

If you wear glasses, keep your present pair as spares and go looking for new designer specs that look good on you.

You can still go out in your cargo pants and stylishly-torn t-shirt, unshaven, with messy hair, as long as the situation warrants it and you wear it well, that is, are totally comfortable. A coffee shop in the artsy part of town is an example of where this look would work nicely. Just don't start looking for every single possible opportunity to define every place you go to as "artsy" because doing so just provides an excuse to wear torn jeans and junky old t-shirts.

Changing your clothing habits, like everything else, requires that you give yourself time to adjust to the improved look. Remember that if you've been dressing down for many years, it will take more than a few days or weeks to get used to and begin appreciating the benefits of dressing with more care and attention to the colors which best suit you, the styles which best fit your body type, and the fits which help make you your best at home, at work or out on a date.

If you look good, you feel good. That's no cliché.

Accessorize

Wearing nice clothes is a start, but to complete the visual picture you should wear a couple of accessories. My favorites are a nice watch and a rope or bead necklace, but you can go much further and still be tasteful.

Why wear a watch when clocks are everywhere, in your cell phone, on electronic signs, in your car's sound system? A nice watch will look good, and adds a bit of asymmetry to your look. Never buy a new wristwatch by yourself. Bring a close friend whose taste you trust to a jeweler who has a large wristwatch department. Avoid the trend toward monster (44mm+ diameter) wristwatches because few men can pull off such large pieces. Most men look their best – in short sleeves, long sleeves, casual dress, business dress or formal dress – wearing wristwatches between 39mm-42mm in size. An alternative to a watch is a plain or woven wrist band.

I joined a beach volleyball team, and all the guys decided to wear a bead necklace (with the idea of unity, i.e., team spirit). At first the idea seemed completely foreign to me, and a little immature. But I bought one, and started wearing it all the time, even to work. Some people outside of the team complimented me on my 'new look.'

The more unusual the accessory, the greater the likelihood it will be a conversation starter. People may even approach and ask you about it. Have a good story or anecdote to tell them. If you only say *I just bought it because it looked good in the store* they will be bored, but if you say it matches your personality (or your after-work personality) they will be intrigued. Shop with a friend who can offer a balancing second opinion with respect to what looks good on you and what suits your physical presence, complexion and interests.

Stepping out of old habits moves you closer to the person you strive to be.

Hair: Style or Shave it off?

Lots of guys don't pay much attention to their hair. Try going to a decent stylist, one you haven't visited before, and ask their opinion on your present hairstyle. Let them do what they want with your hair (e.g., going for the 'messy' style can look great). If you are balding, a lot of guys look better with their hair very short or even completely shaved off. Combine this with a goatee and a necklace.

I recognize this may be a huge change, one you may be reluctant to do. But following through will be symbolic – it will represent the new person you are releasing from his former prison.

Facial Hair

Generally, goatees and the unshaven look are favored these days by women, followed by the clean shaven look. Full beards are the least favored. Of course, fashion changes periodically, and everyone is different. It is possible you may look better with a full beard or clean shaven than you do otherwise. Try making a change, and see how others react.

Don't forget to own the change; act and feel like it is a great new look for you. This will reinforce it in other's perceptions as they subconsciously read your confidence.

Body Language & Posture

Take note of how you stand while waiting in line somewhere. Do you look at the ground, shoulders slumped? Do you try and take up as little space as possible? Do you always have your hands in your pockets, or your arms folded across your chest? All of these habits transmit low self esteem or insecurity.

Try standing straight, with your shoulders pulled back (though don't overdo the shoulders bit – it can look unnatural; practice in front of a mirror). Look around at people, things of interest, etc. Don't be completely motionless like a statue; gaze around slowly, taking in the surroundings and absorbing information about where you are and who is present. Don't jut your head forward; bring it back in line with the rest of your body, tilting it back slightly.

Don't Fidget

Whether sitting or standing, absent-mindedly tugging at your clothing, touching your face, or scratching your leg or arm all transmit unease. Most of us demonstrate quirks such as these when we're alone, but if you are in a job interview or at a social gathering, fidgeting, shifting your weight, darting your eyes or avoiding eye contact prompts others to see you as at the very least uncomfortable, at worst shifty or untrustworthy.

If you are speaking to someone and the conditions aren't perfect (e.g., if it's too hot, or you have an itch, or something is irritating your eye) you may be tempted to try and make yourself more comfortable by loosening your collar, scratching that itch, blinking your eyes excessively, etc. Resist the temptation; try and endure the discomfort until you disengage from the interaction to get to a private corner or bathroom and adjust your collar, scratch that itch or splash some water into your eyes to clear up whatever is bothering them.

Working on your Walk

Now that you have decent clothes, if you aren't used to getting out and walking your neighborhood, open the door and do so. Consider driving or taking transit to a mall or area you don't normally frequent. Excursions such as this (outside your area) might be psychologically easier, since there is less chance of running into an acquaintance that has a preconceived picture of you. Walking around a new locale, nobody knows you are shy – unless your body language betrays you.

Shy people tend to walk one of two ways; stiffly, as though they are feeling all eyes on them, or timidly, as if they are trying to hide. A stiff walk (where your arms and every other part of your body except your legs are virtually motionless) comes across as robotic. A timid walk (eyes and head down, shoulders slumped, a small gait) comes across as weak. Both types reinforce the negative, self-conscious feelings you have, and are not attractive to anyone who happens to glance your way.

One of the best walks I've seen on screen is that of Sean Connery. Buy or rent any of his earlier movies, especially the Bonds – and study his walk. It is unhurried, fluid, yet purposeful. It might be described as 'gracefully masculine.' Notice his subtle head, shoulder and arm movements. Even when he's under fire he jogs, never runs (not that you should emulate that particular behavior if you are shot at; duck and cover might be advisable if you can't run). Note that Connery was a serious bodybuilder for many years, beginning in 1950, and before that had worked as a lifeguard among other things. The point is, if you're not exercising regularly you're not in tune with your body and you'll have a harder time figuring out and practicing a balanced and confident walk that eventually becomes second nature to you.

A similar walk to Connery's is that of Eric Braeden. He starred in a few movies in the 1960s and 70s, one of my favorites being *Colossus: The Forbin Project,* in which he plays the inventor of a supercomputer that ends up taking over the world. It's another example of a confident man that projects high social status with the simple act of walking through a doorway. Braeden is better known as Victor Newman on the daytime soap *The Young and the Restless,* making women of all ages (viewers and co-stars alike, probably) pay close attention every weekday afternoon.

Improving your walk won't happen overnight, but this is where having a new wardrobe helps – it can almost make you feel like a new person. Have a friend videotape you walking outside, or set up a video camera in your house. Maybe your friend would be interested in learning self-improvement exercises with you (provided he is open and enthusiastic about the idea). Again, don't be discouraged though if he quits – you are more driven than he is, and will continue to make an effort at self-improvement long after he gives up and goes back to his four-hour-a-day videogame habit.

The key to improving your walk (and to improving every other aspect of yourself as you will soon learn further into this book) is to not give a damn. I don't mean you should walk around with a bad attitude, but that you should develop a bit of an *I don't care what others think* outlook. Clear your mind of obstructions caused by worrying about how others think you look so that you can relax and rid yourself of physical tension.

The tenser you are, the more you will stand out as someone who is uncomfortable, and you will inspire feelings of indifference from others. If you simply go for a walk to enjoy yourself, take in the sights, and develop a relaxed stroll, you will not appear self-conscious. With practice, as your walk becomes more and more confident, this will help improve your personality as a whole. Eventually you may gain more admiring glances from women.

Facial Expressions

I'm not a bad looking guy, but I've learned that on those rare occasions when my face is completely relaxed (e.g., when I'm tired or very preoccupied), I look as if I'm overly serious, which is not the impression I want to make. So I've learned to compensate by raising my eyebrows slightly, and giving myself an almost-smile expression. This brightens up my face a bit and as a side benefit I've had some women smile at me on the street as I've walked past them.

A slight smile can give you a sense of self-assuredness. Don't overdo it though – walking around with a big grin all the time isn't a good idea. Save the big smiles for greeting people (even if you aren't exactly thrilled to see them, greeting with a smile makes them feel good, and can improve their attraction of you).

Giving a woman a friendly smile as you pass on the street usually prompts one of two reactions: a return smile, or an avoidance of eye contact. Don't take it personally if most women do not return your smile; she may be involved or otherwise not interested, as shy as you, tuned too keenly to the latest depressing news story about how unsafe the streets are, thinking about work or family or who knows what else. If you go out and smile at a hundred women and none return your smile, there are probably other issues at play, such as your dress or body language.

Eye Contact

This one can be a bit tricky, because an appropriate level of eye contact in one situation can be inappropriate in the next. On the one hand, in any situation it is good to maintain some eye contact (as opposed to looking at the ground or having your eyes quickly dart away if someone looks at you), but on the other hand you don't want to stare at people.

If you're walking down the street and see an attractive woman in the distance walking towards you, don't automatically lock on her eyes. If you do so, as she comes closer she will likely be unnerved by your stare. Wait until she is within a few paces, and then glance at her eyes with a slight smile. It is usually more effective to look at her through the corner of your eye rather than turning your head to face her directly.

Women won't mind if you look into their eyes for a few seconds (especially if it is accompanied with a smile), but any longer than that can make them feel uncomfortable (unless she smiles back, in which case the game is on).

In later sections I go into detail about approaching women directly, but sometimes smiling at a woman on the street is a good opener for conversation. If a smile is returned, a man can consider stopping as he's passing the woman. If she stops too, he should offer a small compliment and then be silent and await a reply. If her body language turns her toward the man and she responds with a thank you or some other positive response, conversation can begin even if it's "You look like an interesting person. I'm taking a break from my day to sit down for a cup of coffee. Would you join me?"

We could all use some more eye contact in our lives. It has a way of generating connections between people, and when done correctly it can build comfort level and eventual intimacy. As long as eye contact is welcomed, the longer it is maintained, the more intimate the experience, but of course this is only effective if the person is open to it in the first place. Experiment with different degrees of eye contact with women – if there is a mutual attraction, extended eye contact can increase that attraction. For women you don't know, looking at their eyes, and then looking away briefly, then back to their eyes is flirtatious.

Generally, when talking with a woman you should maintain eye contact for about three-quarters of the time when you are speaking, and almost as much when she is speaking. You can glance down at her mouth a few times, then back to her eyes, but if it is an extended conversation don't completely fixate on her face – take in the surroundings every so often, then return to her eyes.

The workplace is a different story, because a certain level of professionalism is expected. Brief eye contact as you pass coworkers in the hall is perfect; staring at them as you pass is unnerving, even if you know them fairly well.

With people you know, you should maintain at least some eye contact during conversations. Look into their eyes as they are speaking – it will show you are focused on what they are saying, which tells them you are interested. Looking away too often makes you appear distracted and uninterested. Keep in mind that as men we are hard-wired to detect aggressive behavior in other males, and staring is considered aggressive or arrogant, so looking away about 50% of the time to collect your thoughts is good practice.

You can maintain eye contact much longer with women, especially if there is a mutual attraction.

The Handshake

We've all experienced it. You shake hands with someone giving your usual firm grip, and they present a wilting, weak hand. It gives you an impression of them – a negative one. Always give a firm grip, but tailor your grip to the person. You don't want to crush your elderly aunt's hand, but if the person is in decent shape they will appreciate a firm handshake.

One of my pet peeves is someone that at the beginning of a hand-shake is too quick to close their hand, grasping the tips of my fingers in their fist (when this happens I want to slap them about the head with my other hand, but I resist that temptation). You don't commence the grip until each person's webbed area between thumb and forefinger is touching. Look the person in the eye, and smile with your greeting.

When introduced to women make a point of shaking their hand, with a grip that is slightly less firm than you would with a man, without mak-ing it weak or wilting. Look into her eyes and smile as you say hello. If the two of you are experiencing pleasant eye contact (with a smile) you can hold her hand a moment longer than you would with a man.

If at a social gathering don't stand or walk around with a cold drink in your right hand because when you transfer the drink to your left in order to shake hands, your right hand will be cold.

Assignment #3:

Improve your Look

Make the fundamental life changes as outlined above. These obviously won't happen overnight, but make a commitment and follow through.

- Improve your grooming habits
- Get a stylish haircut (or shave your head!)
- Buy some modern clothes (with the help of sales staff) at more than one store
- Accessorize your look
- Add fluidity to your walk; stroll as if you don't have a care in the world

Case Study: Body Language and "Selling Yourself"

Earlier I mentioned my success with a telephone sales job during my time at university. Through word of mouth I was offered another similar job for the city's annual film festival that needed advertising for its printed program schedule. The people running the festival were very overworked individuals that needed an experienced salesperson, and once hired I went to work to once again set a sales record.

This job meant making more face-to-face sales visits, and without exception I went in with enthusiasm, greeting potential clients with a genuine smile, giving them a firm handshake, and engaging in friendly conversation about the nature of their business and what sort of advertising they had done in the past.

My body language was strong and I was energized with the prospect of making a sale, but I also believed in the product, and genuinely enjoyed talking to local business owners. With very few exceptions they were honest, likable people that were open to talking business with me.

But after that I was hired by another group that was publishing a monthly coupon magazine, and I didn't do very well. What had changed?

Let me backtrack for a second. My university and film festival employers were honest individuals that were contributing to the community, and had set fair prices for businesses advertising in their publications. This came through in my interaction with clients – I was working for an outstanding group of people, I believed in the product, and I believed any business that advertised with them got excellent value for their money.

With the coupon book, I immediately felt a disconnect with those running the show. Their magazine was mainly ads with little informative content, and the rates were on the expensive side. Their distribution was spotty, and they didn't seem to give much consideration to businesses that might advertise with them. Plus, as a group they didn't seem to have much substance, caring more about money than the community.

The clients I had so much success with in the past weren't giving me any business, mostly (I realized later) because of my body language and lack of enthusiasm for the product. I realized advertising in this magazine wouldn't be good value for my clients, and subconsciously my heart wasn't into making the sale.

I wasn't my usual enthusiastic self. I smiled less, made less eye contact, and had lost my confident stride. My shoulders slumped. I didn't want to be in the business of selling inferior goods to nice people, so I quit after a couple of days, without having made a single sale.

This shows the difference your overall contentment with your situation can make. Strive to surround yourself with honest, upstanding people, and avoid those that are negative and selfish. And as long as you believe in yourself, that you have a lot to offer, your body language will reflect that state of mind (with some conscious prompting on your part). If you have little self esteem and think you don't have much to offer anyone, this will be revealed in your body language, and you won't inspire any positive feelings in those you meet.

Keep this in mind for your interactions with people in general, and women in particular. To truly improve your overall presentation, you must not only be conscious of avoiding your old negative body language habits, but of projecting your positive inner self. Concentrate on positive emotions and goals, and what positive things you can offer the other person.

Having something to offer doesn't mean something physical. What you have to offer someone is kindness, attention, and understanding. In any interaction, you are there to make the other person feel good about themselves. This in turn will make you feel good about yourself, which will be reflected in your presentation.

What is your Daily Routine?

Earlier I cited "mundane routines" as an enemy to your progress. I understand the desire to stay indoors. It's safe, it's comfortable, and you don't have to deal with people, with all their unpredictable idiosyncrasies. You don't need to be a recluse to have these feelings, especially if you have encountered your fair share of difficult people.

That being said, we are here to improve your life in all areas, and that includes your outside interactions with others. But first things first – has it been months (or even years) since you have graduated school and don't have a job? Or, were you on track with your career but were laid off? A certain amount of time to regroup is fine, but ensure you are not chronically unemployed out of fear or passivity.

Not having a job is the number two turnoff for women (number one being over thirty and still living in your parent's wood-paneled basement).

Employment Status

If you are stuck in a rut and don't have a job, making an honest effort to find one is the best way to get out of that rut. Getting a source of income is not only a necessary step to financial self-sufficiency, but also for self respect. Men need to work. Be honest with yourself – are you only making a token effort to find work (or a better job)? Are you constantly blaming the economy for your lack of progress? Do you spend more time watching television or surfing online for meaningless tripe than you do in your job search?

If so, stop making excuses. Set a goal to research job prospects for at least two hours a day. Set aside another hour to tailor your résumé to specific employers you are interested in. Draft a good cover letter for each, taking the time to address it to the person that posted the job description (if you are not a good writer ask someone for help or hire a professional service to write a good cover letter for you). Set aside another portion of your day to email your résumé and cover letter.

Only after you have spent some time on the above should you reward yourself with surfing time, but put a cap on your recreational surfing. If you spend more than three hours a day watching television or on the computer, wean yourself down to a reasonable level, say two hours per day (television and surfing time combined) maximum.

Finding a job should be your full-time job. The act of putting in this effort will do wonders for your self-image – you are now putting in real effort to find work, and if you are persistent you will be rewarded.

Doing well in Job Interviews

Don't be late for the interview – arrive about ten minutes early. Read up on the company beforehand, and have a couple of questions ready. Dress in a way that's appropriate for the position, and greet the interviewer with a smile and firm handshake. Don't ask if you'll be expected to work overtime, or if you can have an extra week's vacation.

Maintain an appropriate level of eye contact. This is a professional setting so you don't want to stare, which would project disrespect or an overbearing nature. Neither should you stare at the floor or dart your eyes around, avoiding their gaze. As the interviewer asks you questions, maintain eye contact, but then as you answer the question you can be animated, alternating from eye contact to looking away, and back to eye contact every few seconds.

And as mentioned earlier, keep your fidgeting under control. Don't bounce your knee up and down, scratch your nose, jiggle the change in your pocket, or use fast hand gestures when trying to make a point. If you find it difficult to keep your hands still, clasp them on your lap.

Stay upbeat, sell yourself, and at the end of the interview thank the interviewer for their time.

While this book is not specifically designed to help you find a job, everything I've mentioned so far – positive frame of mind, a clear speaking voice, confident posture and walk, a firm handshake – should be applied to job interviews. Reading subsequent chapters will build on this foundation, and should be applied concurrent with your job search.

For more specific information on working on your resume, crafting a cover letter, and interview etiquette, you should consult specialized material. But again, the principles of interaction are the same here as discussed earlier (and later) on meeting and interacting with people.

Do you Live with your Parents?

If you are able to win women over with your outgoing personality, some women won't mind if you are several years past graduation and still living with your parents. But if you are a reserved person without much dating experience, not having your own place is one more hindering situation that works against you.

If you temporarily moved back in with your parents after college to save money while you pay off your student loans or you have been laid off work and need a cheap place to stay for a while, that's one thing. But know when it is time to venture out on your own again. Living with your parents as an adult can be a stifling experience, one that curtails your social growth.

After being away at college for several years where in the course of your studies you interacted with many other adults and made your own decisions, moving back in with your family after you graduate can be a shock. In your twenties you certainly aren't the same person you were at seventeen or eighteen, but parents tend to treat you like the teenager you were before you left, and you will invariably start resenting them for it. This situation has a way of keeping you from progressing emotionally, and can elevate your stress level (and your blood pressure).

Even if your parents are welcoming of your visiting friends, it is always better for your social life to be living on your own. If you have a full-time job and still live with relatives, give yourself a target date to find your own place. It should be no longer than six months from the day you first read this sentence. Mark it on your calendar.

Some may use the argument that you should stay until you can afford to buy your own house. While this viewpoint has some financial merit, it would better suit someone that already has a rich dating life. You don't, at least not yet. So the 'saving for a house' path may be the worst strategy to follow. One year has a way of turning into two, then three, then four, and before you know it, you are completely settled in and arguing with your parents over which television shows to watch after dinner – and you still don't have a girlfriend.

And owning a house is not always the greatest choice anyway. Look how the financial crisis of 2008 ruined so many new homeowners, who were left with mortgages greatly exceeding the value of their homes and forced many people into bankruptcy. Renting isn't such a bad idea, and many prefer it even during good times, when they can invest the money that would otherwise go to interest payments. Done right, this strategy can be more lucrative than owning a home (and if your rent is reasonable you may still be able to save for eventual home ownership).

So renting (or sharing rent with a trusted room mate) is not a bad idea. Having a room mate can get you used to dealing with people other than family, and will probably widen your social circle as you get to know each other's friends and perhaps even go to the occasional party.

Search for a place in an appropriate area – don't look for an apartment in a sleepy residential area populated with retirees waiting to die (unless you plan to be so socially active you won't be home much, which is a good strategy in any case). Look for a place to live that is on the upswing, with plenty of young people. It's true that the most desirable areas are also the most expensive, but you can get around this somewhat by getting a place that is slightly smaller than optimal, or in a slightly less desirable section that lets you easily travel to some energetic areas of town (e.g., via walking, public transit or a short drive). The worst areas to live are deep in the suburbs or on the fringe of an industrial park. The point is to avoid choosing a place to live that is so far from the action – movie theatres, clubs, restaurants, shopping, friends, meeting places, events, galleries, museums, etc. – that it becomes a huge effort and takes too much time to get there.

Three

GETTING USED to
INTERACTING WITH PEOPLE

Let's say you don't live with your parents and don't consider yourself a recluse. You may still have become addicted to your routine of coming straight home from work every evening, watching television or surfing the internet. Even if you are spending your time on social networking sites, there is no substitute for face-to-face human interaction. As mentioned earlier, Facebook and sites of this ilk should be considered a secondary social outlet, not your primary one.

Even after completing the telephone assignments above, you still may not be comfortable having conversations with women in person. If you have a paralyzing fear of venturing outside and talking to people, ensure you have completed the chapters on developing an online presence and telephone interaction. If you are only mildly fearful of talking to strangers, go shopping. Interact with store clerks. A standard and successful technique often prescribed by therapists is to plan a few 30-60 second conversation topics to use with a store clerk, checkout cashier, store salesperson and new introductions. One minute is generally considered a comfortable limit for two people when checking out with a full carry basket of groceries, asking a clerk for help finding a particular item in a hardware or clothing store, or after an introduction to someone.

When banking, use a real live teller instead of a machine. It may seem simple, but if you are shy the best thing you can do to lessen your social anxiety is to talk to as many people as possible, as often as possible.

Most of us are far too reluctant to talk to strangers. In a small town where everyone knows everyone else you can't walk a block without at least saying hello to a few people. I advocate doing this, even if you live in a big city. I'm not talking about planting yourself in the middle of a crush of people at the train station during the afternoon rush (you would likely be ignored, if not trampled). Instead, walk the mall or a nice street with a vibrant shopping area and browse shops.

The pace should be leisurely, allowing an easy hello as you pass other shoppers (don't concentrate on people that are walking quickly or otherwise disengaged, but on those that are browsing or walking at a slower pace). Give a smile as you do so. Most people will at least smile back, if not also returning your greeting.

Even if you are painfully shy, simply saying "hello" as you pass someone is within your abilities, even at this early stage. You are not under pressure to continue the conversation, or to be interesting or funny. Besides, a smile and a hello can speak volumes anyway. After doing this a few times you will feel a nice, positive vibe coming from others that smile back.

At this stage you do not need to approach women you are attracted to. Older retirees are ideal, because as a group they tend to be very friendly and very willing to talk when approached.

Assignment #4:
Saying "Hello" to Strangers

Go to a mall or retail street, browse shops, anywhere people are milling about at a leisurely pace. Say "hello" to at least five people a day, male or female.

Expanding the Conversation

Turning it up a notch, you can make small talk with people. This is especially easy if you are in a line to buy something or are waiting for service at a bank. The other person is probably bored and wouldn't mind if you struck up a conversation. Topics can be anything, but here are a few ideas:

- Make an observation about the surroundings, such as how slowly the line is moving. While not absolutely necessary, it is better to inject some humor, e.g., "By the time we reach the counter my new shirt will have gone out of style" (say it with a smile).
- The weather; you can make a simple comment on the current conditions (it's hot, cold, rainy, sunny), but it is preferable to add a positive statement to go along with it (rather than complaining about it). For example if you have a nephew, say "I'm glad the weather is nice, my nephew's birthday picnic is this weekend" or make some other true (or almost true) correlation.

Take the opportunity to mention the weather or something remarkable about the surroundings (e.g., a construction project that is slowly shaping up) as often as possible (with different people each time of course) in elevators, line-ups, etc.

Again, if talking to an interesting woman is too intimidating at this stage, keep your small talk directed at people you normally wouldn't date. Ask an older person for their opinion on a nearby restaurant. This is to get you comfortable talking to strangers, which eventually will lead to confidence when talking to attractive women. Remember – you're not trying to pick up someone, but rather practice social skills.

Assignment #5:

Short Conversations with Strangers

When implementing Assignment #4, you may have found one or two people that did more than simply return your hello. Hopefully the conversation was comfortable; if not, go out and repeat this assignment often. Make it a routine to visit the same area (or different area, if feasible) on a regular basis, at lunch time when people are milling about, a couple of nights per week after work and every Saturday or Sunday. Create a new social routine of browsing a different shopping area every weekend, and saying hello to strangers.

- Broaden your hello into small talk with at least five people per weekend, focusing on those you wouldn't be interested in dating. Keep the conversations short for now. Repeat this exercise as much as possible, every weekend, and during your weekday lunch hours.

Assignment #6:
Enroll in Special Interest Courses

Most towns and cities have a community college. The largest towns, medium size and larger cities boast several community colleges, often with campuses in different areas. Most offer high-quality instruction at less than half the cost of degree-granting universities.

Investigate community college courses for subjects that interest you. This puts you in a social situation with people that share that particular interest. Gauge how easy it is for you to start or respond to conversation. If you are completely silent and don't participate in classroom discussions, consider broadening your horizons by taking courses on subjects you have less interest in – maybe a course that is heavily favored by women. The fish-out-of-water experience may force you to ask questions and seek help from classmates.

Going to a more advanced level, start tailoring the courses you take to a more social theme. A good approach here would be to enroll in a public speaking course.

For my own experience in this area, the college that was most convenient for me to attend after work had only one business presentation course, so I took it twice; once in the summer, then again the following winter. The format consisted of a three-hour evening class each week for twelve weeks. We were expected to make three presentations during the twelve weeks. If you weren't presenting, you watched your classmates present.

You may be thinking, *He wants me to do presentations! That's impossible! Doesn't he know I'm too shy?!?*

There are some mitigating factors to giving practice presentations in a classroom setting versus the real thing in a boardroom. First, the other students are there for a reason. They are either extremely shy themselves, or are poor presenters, so you are not alone. Second, your teacher and fellow students are a friendly, understanding audience that will give you some useful pointers. And third, the stakes are low – if you don't give a great presentation you will not be fired or ridiculed. Quite the opposite – you'll receive beneficial critique.

Just like everyone else, you are there for self improvement. If the course is comprehensive enough, the teacher will give you tips and maybe even relaxation techniques that will help calm your nerves before you get up to speak. If not, I have a few here.

- Know your subject. If you are able to choose your own topic, make it one you are familiar with. If the topic is assigned to you and is unfamiliar, ensure you do as much research as possible. In most cases the first presentation is the shortest, maybe five minutes (your second and third presentations will probably be a little longer), so it is not as if you're expected to write a graduate thesis.
- Use 3x5 note cards with the points you want to raise in bullet point form. Don't read entirely from a script. If possible throw in an anecdote from your personal experience. Smile as you deliver it.
- Before each rehearsal, practice deep, slow breathing techniques to relax yourself.
- Practice at home as much as possible, and time yourself. Video (or at least audio) record your performance. In most cases upon playback you will be surprised at how quickly you are speaking. Practice slowing your voice down. Pausing is your friend – what seems like an eternity to you is only seconds to the audience, so if you momentarily lose your place, they probably won't notice.
- When it is time for your presentation, look between people rather than directly at their eyes (however move your eyes from one section of the room to the other, so you appear to be giving attention to the entire room). This may seem strange at first, but it keeps you a little detached from the audience, and can lessen your anxiety. Later as you get more comfortable you can start to establish real eye contact, from person to person (don't stare at one per-

son for long). As your confidence builds, eye contact with your audience makes for a more effective experience for everyone.

- If possible, use visual aids such as a projector, or have some bullet points on the blackboard for reference.
- Don't root yourself in one spot – move about the front of the class, or even into the audience as you speak if it is practical. This can also relax you, but keep your movements slow, deliberate, and comfortable.
- As you wrap up your presentation, smile and thank the audience. They will warm to you for this.

Other courses you could take include leadership or management skills (usually business oriented, but will help your leadership skills no matter what field you are in) and assertiveness programs, again at your local college or community center.

This is an ongoing process – I'm not talking about taking one or two courses and then quitting. Following your interests and becoming proficient at any skill, be it wine making or stand-up comedy, takes dedication and time, and will make you a more interesting person and open up new social opportunities.

If the course pickings are slim, repeat them. You will notice a huge difference in your progress the second time around.

The benefits to this strategy are many. You will be more comfortable in any social group, be it personal or professional, and eventually you will no longer fear speaking up in meetings.

Arts or Community Shows

Check the local university events site for guest speakers, musical performances, plays, and other events you can attend. Also, check the local paper for similar events at your community centre. These will not necessarily require interaction with others, but there will be opportunities for small talk with people before or after the show. It also gets you acquainted with what goes on in your city. This will come in handy if you and a friend (or a date) wish to do something more interesting than usual.

Four

THE ART of CONVERSATION

Communication skills are number one. You can be short, overweight, bald, have an acne problem, walk with a limp or have uncounted other issues, but as long as you have at least a bit of the gift of gab, you will attract people, drawing them in with your charisma. Of course there are stipulations. If you don't have a broad field of interest you may only feel comfortable talking to people that share your particular views, so it pays to develop an awareness of what's going on in the world so you can relate to varied groups of people.

This is another reason I recommend taking courses, entering into a new hobby and (later in the book) travel. All of these things give you new life experiences that build your emotional intelligence while giving you lots to talk about to family, friends, and strangers alike.

Good conversationalists tell about some of their experiences using engaging language and brief descriptions which stay on point. They listen actively to what others have to say, rarely interrupt anyone, and maintain relaxed eye contact. The general effect is that they show respect for what others have to say, no matter how important or inconsequential, and in that way help other people feel confident too.

First Impressions Count

Within the first few moments of meeting you, a person forms an opinion. They take note of how you are dressed, your body language (if you are slouched or tense, or confident and at ease), and how you address people (if you shake hands and smile, or nervously look away immediately after the introduction).

Much of this first impression is laid down in the person's mind before you even speak, so if you have a relaxed confident posture at all times, keep your head up with a smile and have a direct gaze, people are apt to judge you positively, and be more likely to approach you.

Match your Mood to the Room and the People

Take a reading on the overall vibe of the venue (be it a small get-together in someone's living room, or a larger party in a rented space) and try to match it. Sure, if there are a lot of loud people telling jokes it may be pointless for the reserved person to emulate that behavior, but as long as you stay attentive with relaxed body language (as opposed to being an expressionless brooder) you will blend in.

At the other end of the scale, some intimate gatherings are very low-key (probably more your style). Again, pay attention to what is going on and keep yourself approachable; the worst thing you can do is sit off to the side alone staring down at your drink or smart phone. Make attempts to join conversations.

Catch someone's eye – preferably a woman's eye – smile, and nod in greeting. Offer your name as an introduction, accept the woman's name in response. Then state truthfully that you don't know anyone present very well and feel a bit like a duck out of water, but say this confidently, not as if you are hoping she will talk to you. If you project a relaxed confident manner people will be far more likely to stay and chat. If you get a positive response from the woman, engage in conversation (some tips are outlined below).

Joining a Conversation

If you are standing beside a group and you overhear something that piques your interest, you then have an opportunity to break in.

Let's say you love comedy movies. If somebody in the group mentions that they saw the latest big comedy film, you could say "Excuse me, I couldn't help overhearing what you said about the movie, I'm thinking of going to see it, was it any good?"

After they reply it helps if you can have a follow up comment, such as mentioning a similar film you saw earlier.

Conversations can be easier in planned events such as birthdays, holiday get-togethers, weddings, etc., where you will know some of the guests. Before attending, take note of who you will be seeing, and recall what their interests are. Have a couple of topics ready that you could use as conversation starters, be it from your own experience or theirs.

Keep abreast of news and current events. Read up on topics that your friends or colleagues enjoy. You don't need to become an expert, but if you know of any major developments in their area of interest (a sports team has paid millions for a new player; there is a regime change in the Middle East, etc.), they will likely be interested to talk about it.

Don't Reply with Only One Sentence

When talking to someone you just met it is almost inevitable you will be asked where you are from. The easy answer is to reply in one word or sentence: "I'm from Toronto," and then leave it at that. Unfortunately this forces the other person to carry the conversation, which may stall.

Instead, add some detail to your answer: "I'm from Toronto. I grew up here (or have been here x years), how about you?" This adds to the discussion and invites participation from the other person.

Do the same when somebody asks you what you do for a living. Don't just say "I'm an accountant," or "I'm an engineer." Flesh it out by adding true details, something like "I'm an accountant doing freelance work for a law firm. They just merged with another firm so we're very busy. Never a dull moment for us accountants!"

Don't Ask What They Do

Incidentally, though I'm asked what I do all the time, I generally don't ask other people. Why not? Just in case they are unemployed, or if they are a stay-at-home Mom or Dad, which they may not wish to reveal. It's better to let them volunteer that information, if they so choose.

Delay Saying "I Did That Too"

It can be a bonding experience when you find out you have something in common with the other person, but over the years I've learned that being a good listener can make the experience much better rather than if you jump in exclaiming your common interest too quickly.

For example, if you have been to Ireland and a person happens to mention the wonderful vacation they spent there, don't immediately jump in saying "I've also been to Ireland." Let them continue their story for a time describing the sights, people, atmosphere, and various destinations the visited. They won't cut themselves off prematurely just because you've been there, and will continue to relate their experience unimpeded.

Wait for a good time to jump in, perhaps after they finish an anecdote about a certain aspect of the trip, then mention you have that destination in common. If they ask you why you didn't mention it sooner, say you loved their description and wanted to hear them finish.

They will likely smile and ask you about your experience, and the two of you can continue the conversation based on that shared interest.

What if You are Super Shy?

If you are extremely shy and break out into a cold sweat at the thought of talking to anyone at a social gathering, there are a few techniques that will help. First, repeat Assignment #4 (saying hello to strangers) as often as you can. If this is a new behavior for you, the only way to get any measure of comfort is to do it repeatedly.

There are certain universal truths about having a good conversation, and paramount is the ability to relate to the experience being described by the other person. On the other hand, if your Dungeons & Dragons hobby is not shared by most of your relatives and their friends, it will not benefit you to talk about that subject, which will be judged as boring.

Some mundane subjects like the weather are fine if there has been an unusual weather pattern. Other topics you can tap into are the well-being of a person's relatives, e.g., *How's the family? Has your brother finished his degree?* People usually enjoy talking about family events such as upcoming graduations, weddings, etc.

An added difficulty of being extremely reserved is that the longer your conversational statement is, the greater chance you have to become nervous and stammering. So with that in mind, keep the statement short.

If you have trouble thinking of statements on the spot, write down three or four and memorize them. If you think your mind will go blank the next time you are out, enter them into your mobile phone's memo pad, and read them while at the gathering on the pretext of reading an email. Don't spend much time with your phone though. It is bad form to sit there and pay more attention to your phone than to people.

As you get more comfortable with longer statements, you can relate a very short story, again on a subject that people can relate to.

Here's an example. A windows & doors company recently contacted me by phone, and offered to send a representative over to my place to give me a no-obligation estimate for replacing some of my windows for a price that would be valid for two years. The guy came over, examined the house windows, sat down at my dining room table to discuss their products and crunch some numbers.

He ended up giving me a price, and wanted to get a work order from me right away. I said I do not make spur of the moment decisions, and would give him an answer in a couple of weeks. At that, he gave me an exaggerated expression of sadness, and remarked how he was having to "drive all the way home without a sale."

That's what some salespeople do – they try and make you feel as if they have done you a great favor so you feel obligated to give them the sale.

If you add some energy to the conversation, it becomes 100% more effective:

"The guy got this pouty look on his face. I swear, he was ready to cry right there and then!"

There. I just came up with a conversation topic that any homeowner can relate to. You can do the same thing, but to ensure you will not go blank write down a few experiences you have had that would be good conversation topics.

Make the Conversation about Them

Make the conversation event about the other person – be unselfish, and stop thinking about how you look or sound. If you focus on your perceived shortcomings, you will not only be sabotaging yourself, but also short-changing the other person by not truly focusing on them.

Always take an interest in the other person. Ask about what they did on the weekend (or would like to do the following weekend).

How to Keep the Conversation Going

If you struggle on what to say, you can repeat the last word or line your conversational partner mentioned, which usually prompts them to go into more detail. For example, if someone says "I didn't have much of a problem with most of my courses, but the last one was really difficult."

You could simply reply, "Difficult?"

This opens the door for them to explain why the course was a problem for them and what they did to get through it.

If a person comments that they really liked the movie and then stops talking, you could repeat *you really liked it?* It's an invitation for them to continue. They may explore what aspects of the movie they enjoyed. Keep doing this and the person will carry most of the conversation. As long as you remain focused and have good eye contact they will view the experience positively, believing you are an attentive listener and even a great conversationalist, even though you may not have said much.

Be an Insider

Each sport, profession, and enthusiast hobby has its own terms for describing its common or important aspects. For instance, in skiing, those bumps you see on the intermediate to expert hills are called moguls. If you are talking to a skier and ask them if they like to ski over the bumps, they may roll their eyes and change the subject (or be unenthusiastic about continuing the present conversation). On the other hand if you ask them if they like skiing the moguls they will naturally warm to you as someone that knows something about their sport.

As mentioned, it pays to be well rounded and well read. You don't need to be an expert in everything, but even trying a new activity once will usually be enough to give you a grasp of the basics. Shake up your routine; instead of riding your bike every weekend, take a sailing lesson. Even if you don't meet any sailors in the future, at the very least if you enjoyed the lesson it will give you something to talk about the next time you are at a social gathering. And if you really enjoyed the lesson, it may prompt you to take it up as a new hobby.

Keep the Conversation Upbeat

You can complain about your bank charges and data fees being high (everyone can relate to those topics), but otherwise keep your negative comments to a minimum, and never complain about someone that isn't present. You don't want to get the reputation of being a downer, gossiper or braggart.

You may be tempted to reveal something exciting in an attempt to sound attractive or impressive, but this can backfire, especially with people you just met. Don't talk about how you were arrested for public drunkenness in college, that your best friend is cheating on his wife, or how you got such a fat bonus this year that you splurged on a top-of-the-line this or that.

Instead, mention accomplishments that mutual acquaintances have made, festivals you have enjoyed, interesting news you have heard, and so on. If you do this people will associate you with positive thoughts.

Neither should you be venturing into other's personal finance areas, asking how much money they make or how much their property is worth. That's their own private business.

You may be privy to some tidbit of information about a person that a mutual friend revealed. This does not mean you should necessarily broach that subject to the person. For example, suppose your friend mentioned earlier that Steve, a fellow guest at the party is an avid cyclist and just spent $7000 on a new bike. It would be rude for you to approach Steve with *wow, I heard you spent $7000 on your bike!* This is a tactless way to broach what may be a sensitive subject; you wouldn't mention how much they paid for their house, would you?

A better tactic would be to say *Steve, I hear you are really into cycling and just bought a new bike. How do you like it?*

If the information is serious (e.g., their relationship ended, they lost their job) you shouldn't mention it at all unless they volunteer it first.

How to Get Invited to Parties

Many of us would love to widen our social circle of friends, e.g., get some new friends in addition to the same people we've hung out with since high school. One of the easiest ways to do this is to follow the advice in Assignment #6, and enroll yourself into several evening or special interest courses.

This is more effective if you choose courses that are several weeks in length, or better yet part of a series, such as acting, language, or any other subject in which the majority of students will be expected to take the next level. The social benefits are less likely in a career oriented subject like database management – choose your courses wisely. As you move ahead as a group you will likely bond with the rest of the class.

There will usually be one or two social butterflies that love to throw parties, and sooner or later they will organize a get-together for the entire class (if the class was fairly small), or for your smaller study group. Sometimes the host will invite their own friends to the party, so there may be some new faces you haven't seen.

On the off chance that everyone in the group is low-key and doesn't organize a party, you have two choices: organize one yourself, or find an additional course to take in which you will be with another crowd. In any case it is recommended that you find more than one subject of interest; devoting two nights per week (one to each group) will not only keep you active, it allows you to interact with different people.

If you wish to organize something but are too self-conscious about having people over to your place, you can suggest an after-dinner gathering at a pub or an activity, such as a boat cruise in the local harbor or some other tourist-type activity that people normally would not do on their own (it is fun to play tourist in your own city).

In an earlier chapter I recommended volunteering for a charity or political organization as a way to help you get comfortable on the phone. This is also a great way to kick-start your social life, and there are other jobs you can do at the head office besides being on the phone, such as administrative work.

If you already have a career and/or a degree, don't think that administrative work at a charity or political party office is beneath you – if it is for a cause you believe in and will have a positive effect on the community, it will be worthwhile spiritually as well as socially.

These organizations usually have some sort of social event every few weeks as a show of appreciation for their members. It's also a good way to network if you are looking for a career change because many volunteers you'll interact with have unrelated careers.

Keep in mind that you must be in regular attendance to be recognized as part of the ensemble. If you skip most classes or meetings you may not qualify for an invitation.

It is good practice to bring something to a private social gathering, especially if it is a dinner party. Depending on the setting, this could be a bottle of wine, appetizer, a desert, or other item you deem appropriate.

Party Etiquette

You can always tell the shy, awkward people at a party from their body language and mannerisms; they tend to lurk in a corner with arms folded or sit off to the side away from the other guests. They generally try to occupy themselves with food and drink, or spend time on their smart phone, head down, texting away.

When you first enter the room it is tempting to avert your gaze from the crowd and make your way to the refreshment table. But this immediately sends a message that you are not comfortable. A better strategy is to briefly pause at the entrance and survey the room with confident body language and a smile, with arms at your sides, not crossed or with your hands in your pockets. Let people see your face and good mood.

Take note of people you may want to meet. A confident person can introduce himself even to a group he doesn't know, but if you are not feeling this bold you can do so to a person that is by themselves. You can open by introducing yourself and asking them if they are from the area. Throughout the engagement remember the earlier sections on body language, eye contact, and handshakes.

Holding food in one hand and a drink in the other puts a barrier between you and anyone else you may wish to talk to. It also makes it more difficult for people to approach. You can't shake anyone's hand, and you may be munching away, unable to talk. It's best to eat before arriving at the party so you visit the refreshment table sparingly, if at all. However if you meet someone and strike up a mutually interesting conversation, one of the things the two of you can do together is to hit the food and drink tables.

Stick to Safe Topics

During a time in my life when I was active in volunteering for my local constituency I was at a social gathering in which the hosts were also active in their community, and some of the guests happened to be affiliated with different political parties. While getting myself a drink a man approached me and introduced himself as belonging to a rival party to the one I belonged to. Within seconds of the introduction he proclaimed that the leader of my party (the governing party) was an "idiot."

I responded by saying he was entitled to his opinion, whereby he launched into all the bad policies of the current government. What made his behavior all the more baffling was that he had his ten year-old daughter by his side. For all this guy knew, I could have been some unstable political fanatic, ready to punch a rival in the mouth at the slightest provocation. I ignored him and walked away, to the visible relief of the hostess, who had been watching at a distance.

I was amazed this guy would make such remarks to someone he had just met. This gathering was not intended to be one for spirited political debates, which just underscored the inappropriate nature of his comment. I enjoy a debate as much as the next guy, but sometimes you just want to chill out and be social.

Talking about politics and religion can be perilous, especially among people who are devout or have strong opinions. If you join such a conversation, keep your remarks respectful.

Introducing People

You are talking to your friend at a party, and another friend of yours approaches to say Hi. Your two friends don't know each other. The worst thing you can do is just chat back and forth, alternating between them without any introduction. The second worst thing would be to introduce them by name only, and then leave them to fend for themselves.

The best course of action is to add some detail about each. For instance, you could say *John this is Doug. Doug just got a new job as a pharmacist at a big drug store downtown. Doug, John recently got back from a ski trip at that nice resort you mentioned a while ago.* By offering complimentary information about each person you will prompt additional conversation between the two.

Instantly the two strangers have things to talk about. You can stick around, or excuse yourself with a clear conscience to say hello to that woman at the bar.

What if You Fall into the Frozen Shrimp?

Let's say there is some sort of food or beverage accident, either caused by yourself or another guest, which results in the front of your shirt or pants being covered in fruit punch. You may be tempted to make a big deal of it, and to run to the washroom or the exit. The best course of action is to do nothing.

Well, not quite nothing; you don't want to have bits of fruit hanging off your clothes for the rest of the night. But if you don't make a big deal of it, neither will anyone else. The nearest person (perhaps the person that caused the accident) will likely hand you some napkins to help with the situation. As you clean up, smile, shrug your shoulders, brush off the mess as much as possible, and continue as if nothing happened.

Alternatively, you could make a humorous quip, such as "that's okay, I needed to cool off anyway."

Don't worry about the stain; people realize accidents happen (in fact, sooner or later, they happen to everyone, so chances are most of the people at the party have been in the same situation). This is no big deal, and when people see you shrug it off and be cool instead of reacting negatively or with embarrassment, your status will actually rise, especially with the perpetrator of the mishap, who will be thankful for your calm reaction under pressure.

How to Take a Compliment

Some people get embarrassed when anyone pays them a compliment, perhaps because they fear being seen as too pleased with any praise they get, so they ignore the kind words in an effort to appear unaffected. This is rude. If someone praises one of your accomplishments or your appearance, smile and say *thank you,* or *thanks, that was very nice of you to say,* and then leave it at that.

Don't be reluctant to compliment others on occasion, even if they themselves do not give praise often – as long as it isn't excessive they will appreciate your positive comments, especially when made in public.

Building your Social Proof

This is a similar concept to the earlier strategy (enrolling in evening courses to build your social life), but it deserves its own category.

The reason enrolling in courses is effective (especially courses where most of the students move on to the next level as a group) is that the repetitive meeting and interactions with your peers eventually turns into a bonding experience. A few people bond with others at their day jobs, but this is not likely if you or your colleagues have little in common besides work, or if you don't enjoy your job. Hobbyist evening courses bring together people who share interests, and are generally more fun, so the atmosphere is more conducive to developing friendships.

This atmosphere can also be cultivated in your local café or tavern, especially if it is a smaller, independently owned establishment.

Determine where the most suitable location(s) would be to spend some time after work and weekends. You could have a separate place for each category, for example a pub near your place of employment for relaxing after work, and another place around your neighborhood for weekend brunch. Look for places that appeal to you and have friendly staff, and start frequenting them as a regular. Make a point to smile and be friendly to the staff when ordering. Introduce yourself and make small talk when they aren't busy; greet and address them by their first name.

Be sure to visit about once a week, engaging in small talk each time. Don't overdo it by forcing the conversation, or keeping them from doing their job. Use some of the conversation tips discussed earlier. If you only visit once a month it may not be frequent enough for you to be recognized, especially if there is a different shift working. Larger chain restaurants or bars may be a little too big with a higher number of staff and customers, making this process more difficult.

Humor is valuable here, and you can practice your interactions with women by gently teasing the female servers. If they make a mistake with your order you can immediately say "you're fired," while making eye contact and giving a mischievous smile. For a quip like this to work, timing is crucial. If you wait more than a few seconds or say it with a straight face while looking away, it will come off as rude rather than humorous.

If you become adept at being friendly with the staff, eventually they will greet you with familiarity when you enter, which is great for building social proof with any date you bring. You could also strike up conversations with other regular customers. Women love it when you inspire friendly greetings from others.

Don't be a Cheapskate

Generosity is a noble trait. Some are generous to a fault, lending money and possessions haphazardly to others who may take advantage of their good nature. At the other end of the spectrum are those who are tight-fisted and inhospitable, even towards friends. I'm not going to give advice when it comes to lending money – that topic is a minefield. But when it comes to everyday interactions (buying a round for the group, being hospitable to visitors), you should err on the side of generosity.

For many of us our primary social event is going out to meet friends for food and drink. In North America it is customary to tip in bars and restaurants, usually 15% of the bill before tax. Some people consistently contribute less (e.g., 10%, even if the service was good), leaving their friends feeling they must make up the difference because they don't want the server to be shortchanged. Others are accidentally cheap, that is, when looking at a bill will add 15% tip to the total before tax and then forget the tax, not realizing that in many locals it actually adds up to approximately the same amount as the tip. As a result they covered the bill, but when tax is factored in little or no tip remains. If someone does this repeatedly, one wonders just how 'accidental' their calculation is.

A female acquaintance of mine related a story about how she dealt with her best friend in this circumstance, who despite being a very nice person in most respects was a bit of a tightwad when tipping at restaurants. My acquaintance felt she had to make up for her friend's shortfall (which got very expensive over time). Her solution was to let her friend order first, and then order the same thing or a meal that was priced similarly. When it came to paying the bill, her friend would pull her usual stunt, whereupon my friend would correct her by saying, "Marie, our total comes to the same amount, and so here's how much we owe with tax included, and here's how much with the tip."

It's puzzling that some people can be well-adjusted in most respects but then be obsessed with getting a free ride from others. This is not a good way to treat friends. In addition to the tipping example, this can include nickel & diming people for gas money on shorter trips, never buying a round for your buddy or the group (if it is a ritual that the group sometimes practices, or if they have otherwise been regularly hospitable to you), being on the stingy side when entertaining visitors, or even giving visiting friends the brush-off. Rationalization is common, which is why people such as these never see themselves as cheap and can display this character flaw over many years or even their entire lifetime.

Though your male friends generally won't keep score in the short term, people catch on eventually, and while they may continue your acquaintance, they will tire of the inequity you project and cut down on the number of times they invite you out. So the 'free ride' mentality backfires.

Women notice signs of stinginess far sooner than men, and it is a complete turn-off to them, which can be a leading cause of not getting a second date.

Five

WHAT WOMEN WANT

Before continuing with more advanced assignments, we will examine the differences between men and women, and why it is sometimes difficult for men to understand the best way to attract the opposite sex.

Men and Women are Different

I attended University during the early 1990s, the time when the Politically Correct tidal wave was sweeping North America. One of the predominant ideas in academic and sociological circles was that women and men, aside from the obvious physical differences, were born mentally and emotionally identical, with any psychological or behavioral differences in the sexes only the result of societal conditioning.

I disagree with that hypothesis, as do many modern, authoritative, widely accepted and highly respected studies.

While environmental factors play a part in anyone's development, that is only part of the story. We are the sum total of our biology and chemistry after all, with millions of years of evolution shaping not only our bodies and physical presence, but also our brains with their emotional responses and intelligent processes. It has been proven that the brains of men and women are different in significant ways, both chemically and in their structure (women's brains have a slightly larger, better developed language center, for instance[4]).

Additionally our brains are, among other things, chemical factories, manufacturing and releasing hormones, enzymes, and other neuro- and bio-transmitters into our bloodstream. Some affect our emotions, and thus our behavior. Testosterone and estrogen, the male and female sex hormones, have been clearly shown to affect animal behavior. We are affected as well, though usually not as extremely as some examples in the animal kingdom.

These various internal stimuli shape who we are, and give males and females somewhat different courtship behaviors and goals. Though individuals vary, overall the old clichés are true – while each gender is capable of displaying logic and emotion, women give greater weight to emotion when making a decision, and men rely more on logic.

There are more differences, including how each gender judges a prospective mate. Although personality usually plays a bigger part, men also give great importance to the visual, i.e., how voluptuous her body may be, how smooth her skin is. It serves a purpose – to perpetuate the species, men are pre-programmed to give a preference to young, healthy women who appear most likely to be able to successfully bear children. Many women believe men are superficial because of this, but it is a predetermined evolutionary behavior.

Women have shopping lists of their own – just look at the content of many online profiles in which women list humor, financial security, good looks, style, athleticism, and more as what they desire in a mate. And let's not forget the countless magazine articles published on how a woman can land the man of her dreams. Women are unable to avoid some level of attraction to a man who appears capable of fathering children and providing her with protection and security. A few decades of contemporary sense about equal pay for equal work and legitimately won women's rights don't alter the imperatives which have resulted from hundreds of millennia of perpetuation of the species. Battling evolution is a no-win scenario.

Therefore, it's a pointless exercise of some women to complain about how "awful" men are because of the importance they place on looks and sensuality, or that men are "natural born cheaters" who will always look for a younger specimen to fool around with.

Whenever a new study on infidelity is published, the statistical probability of cheating is so close between the sexes – often about 52% for men, 48% for women – it is clear each gender is far from perfect.

If anything, women employ a much longer shopping list when looking for a mate. But again, there is no point in men complaining that women make snap judgments when rejecting a man. They do, to the detriment of shy guys everywhere, and themselves, since many reserved guys have those desirable qualities that would come to the fore after a few dates. Again, this is determined by evolution. Evolution may have ensured the overall survival of the species, but it can be completely wrong on an individual level, which is why it pays to study this material to help ensure you meet a woman's shopping list needs on the first date.

Women want an emotionally strong man, someone that can provide for and protect her offspring. This is why it is important to many women that the man has a decent job, is stable under pressure, and is assertive. These preferences are so ingrained that even women past child bearing age still want men with these qualities. Some women prefer the man be older than she is, so that he can bring the benefit of his life experience to the table.

Further, women want men who are able to comfortably interact with, or better yet, lead a social group. This also helps ensure the well-being of the family. The ability to influence others, or at least be accepted into the group, shows the man has some influence among his peers. Conversely, a loner that is shunned by the peer group tends to be shunned by women.

Men on the other hand place less importance on a woman's social status or her job, and more importance on appearance and youth. Physical beauty signifies health and the ability to bear children. Physical attractiveness is strongest when we're young, which is why most men prefer women younger than themselves. This does not mean that men don't like a woman with career aspirations, but that most men put less importance on those attributes.

While the characteristics we desire in a mate may be partly instinctive, they are reinforced by the customary differences in the way men and women dress and behave. Most women dress to accentuate their figure. Cleavage has never gone out of style. And look how a man's suit appears to broaden his shoulders – that's no accident of fashion.

Obviously these are not hard and fast rules (since some men date women older than themselves, and some women date underemployed men), but the biological differences go a long way to explaining why most women want confident, intelligent men that are in decent physical condition to protect the family, and men want a nurturing, healthy, youthful partner who can bear children and take care of the emotional needs of the family. There are too many indicators that the differences between the sexes are innate, and not completely manufactured by society.

Many women seem to be intellectually at odds with that reality. While perusing online dating profiles I can't tell you how many times I've read the following: "I don't need a man to complete me; I just want a man to compliment me."

North American society tells women they are supposed to be strong and independent, with a kick-ass career. There is nothing wrong with that, but it makes many women reluctant to admit they need anything, even a life partner. Personally, I am willing to admit that I'd rather be in a relationship than be single, and I don't believe a person is weak for saying so.

You see how trends and negative perception colors a person's outlook? Only in North America will you see this reluctance to accept the differences between men and women. Europeans tend to recognize and celebrate the differences between the sexes, while North Americans tend to suppress them.

Why Women Like Bad Boys

In the name of equality, North American culture sometimes suppresses the differences between the sexes, but as we've discussed that doesn't mean the preferences don't exist. Here are some synonyms for the word Masculine:

Strong
Bold
Resolute
Virile

Here are some for the word Feminine:

Sensitive
Gentle
Soft
Tender

They fit perfectly with our ideas of the ideal man and woman, re-spectively. You can add a few more for each yourself, though I will just add some for women: *attractive, emotional, seductive* . . . you get the idea.

Women want bold men. Or if that word is too far away from where you are right now, they want decisive men. They want a man that is not afraid to take the lead and make decisions. This doesn't mean they want a tyrant that always wants his way, but someone that is not wishy-washy or tentative in their actions.

If you are a self-described nice guy and don't think there's anything wrong with that, be honest – do you bring any excitement to women's lives? Do you ever playfully tease a woman, or are you always agreeing with her? Are you able to talk to her like you talk to your friends, or are you always smiling and doing her favors?

You are probably displaying the type of behavior women want in a friend, but not in a lover. If you have been displaying these traits for a long time, you must unlearn them and stop being the nice guy, instead working towards being an assertive man. You need to understand this concept and adopt a more resolute outlook. *And stop judging women neg-atively for wanting excitement.* That only reveals you as bitter with an unwillingness to adopt a more adventurous attitude.

This applies to all your behaviors. Again, this does not mean you must become a jerk, but rather a man who leads, has a purposeful stride, a res-olute voice, a steady gaze, a sincere confident smile. All of this equals masculinity. Add to that spontaneity, humor and the ability to playfully tease, along with the resolve to not acquiesce to her every request (i.e., be a challenge to her) and you have a potent mix that almost every wo-man on the planet finds attractive.

Moreover, most women like sexually assertive men. This means know-ing when to escalate to a kiss, and taking the lead in the bedroom.

Now apply any of the feminine traits, and what was positive in a woman becomes negative in a man. Women may say they want a sensitive, tender man, but this is only partly true. They want a man that is masculine, but still capable of being gentle when warranted, e.g., a man that can be romantic and give gentle kisses, be sympathetic to a crisis her family might be going through, etc.

A man whose primary personality characteristics are less masculine (overly soft), including being subservient to most people (in posture and behavior), and who is indecisive, meek, overly agreeable, does not pursue goals and has little ambition, will be very unattractive to women.

When you go back to the earlier chapters on style, developing a confident walk and handshake, and having a clear, decisive speaking voice, it starts to make sense. Those attributes not only help give you confidence, but they also make you more attractive to women.

Have a Temper? Get Rid of It!

Being assertive or even a 'bad boy' does not mean getting angry at others. Some people take out their frustrations on and attempt to dominate those they feel they can take advantage of. Extreme examples are an overbearing caregiver (towards children or the elderly), bullying at work (towards subordinate or peer coworkers) and abusive spousal relationships. Abusers can be male or female.

It is important to differentiate between anger and rage. Anger is an emotion that all of us experience and express from time to time, and is warranted under some circumstances. But we can get angry and still be in control, and without being abusive towards others. Rage on the other hand is out of control sometimes violent anger, and can include screaming or making threatening gestures so that others fear for their safety. Unless you are defending someone from a physical attack this behavior is never justified.

Other examples of excessively angry people are those who frequently:

- Smash inanimate objects (especially if done in front of people, for the intimidation factor)
- Have violent road rage

- Yell at others for accidental errors
- Exhibit overbearing or controlling behavior in an effort to get others to conform to certain wishes or beliefs (by using manipulation, ridicule, ultimatums or threats)

Getting angry at people for small or accidental transgressions, or belittling those who don't conform to your viewpoint is a sign of weakness. Having little self-control or an overbearing nature is not noble or attractive. Nobody expects you to be an emotionless robot, just to have the ability to exercise self control in difficult situations and not take out your frustrations on others.

One of the best compliments an ex-girlfriend paid me was to say that I made her "feel safe." When I asked her to elaborate she mentioned that I didn't feel the need to get angry with difficult people, though I was assertive when needed, and she felt protected when in my presence. That's not to say I never get angry, but I make an effort to keep my anger in check and try not to overreact in difficult situations. Some guys lose their temper too quickly, and it has the effect of making them look emotionally immature. It's always best to be stable under pressure.

Dealing With Aggressive People

Though both Aggressiveness and Assertiveness imply forcefulness, the World English Dictionary describes Assertive as *"confident and direct in claiming one's rights or putting forward one's views."*

If you are in a discussion with someone who is being a little too pushy in trying to get you to agree with their opinion, the best course of action is to politely listen while they get their point across, then say:

"I understand what you are saying, but I feel differently because…"

Thus you present your own argument in a reasoned, calm manner. This works favorably with the vast majority of people you will encounter but some won't respect your right to disagree, becoming derisive as they push their opinions (or 'suggestions'), expecting you to capitulate.

Or they become aggressive. The same dictionary defines Aggressive as *"characterized by or tending toward unprovoked offensives, attacks, invasions, or the like; militantly forward or menacing."*

A fair, balanced individual strives to be assertive and fair, not aggressive and selfish in his dealings with others. Some people are competitive at all costs or use strong-arm tactics to get what they want, be it through emotional outbursts, manipulation, insults or physical intimidation.

If someone yells at you for any reason, your first instinct may be to either yell back at them or retreat to avoid the conflict. Though neither of those is ideal, every situation is different, so you will need to consider the surroundings, the person's history, and the risk of remaining in the area. Usually the best course of action is to stand your ground, look the person in the eye as they are yelling, and say nothing for the period their voice is raised. If the incident involves a stranger, you have no idea what the person is capable of. Again, every situation is unique, but if possible it is wise to err on the side of caution and remove yourself from the area if you sense a danger.

Face to face or on the telephone, a tactic used by successful customer relationship specialists is to say directly to an irate, cursing or yelling individual, "You cannot speak to me like that. It is insulting and rude. Speak to me reasonably and courteously. If you cannot do so then we cannot continue." Having made such a statement, you must be prepared to stand your ground and actually terminate the conversation, showing someone to the door if necessary, hanging up the phone, or leaving the conversation and the place yourself.

If it is a person you know, judge for yourself if asking them to calm down will have the desired effect (it obviously depends on the person's history). Otherwise, don't be in any hurry to reply. Give them a few minutes to get themselves under control. Once they are calm, tell them in a normal conversational tone that their action was overbearing and inappropriate (saying nothing only invites them to continue this behavior in the future). In some cases this will prompt them to do a little self-reflection, but on the other hand some people cannot be reasoned with, exhibiting a pattern of projecting blame for their aggressive temper onto others, perhaps even using this as an opportunity to yell at you yet again.

Habitual screaming at people is abuse and is never justified, and not something you should allow yourself to be subjected to.

Being a Challenge to Women

The number one way that guys blow it with a woman is by showing too much interest in her.

Imagine for a moment a typical adoring fan of an opposite-sex movie celebrity. The fan need not be obsessive, just someone that has more than a passing interest, and substantial affection for the individual. Should they happen to meet on the street, the interaction might go like this:

Fan: "Oh, it's really you! I love your movies! You have so much talent! I'm a huge fan! May I have your autograph? And, um, would you like to go for a coffee sometime?"

The adoring fan followed his first instinct – to praise and be nice to the celebrity, the subject of his desire. After all, he's thinking *who wouldn't like to be around a nice person that praises you?*

Too bad his instinct was completely wrong. In fact, if anything his behavior ensured the celebrity would not in a million years ever have coffee with him.

This is because the adoring fan did not project any value or status, and gave no reason for the celebrity to take him up on his offer. Why would the celebrity drop everything and have a coffee with the adoring fan? What's in it for the celebrity?

The fan went into the exchange putting the celebrity on a pedestal, treating her as if she were this perfect, attractive specimen. The fan has given up all of his status and power, simply handing it over in one sentence. Further, you can probably guess the body language of the fan; he likely had a subservient posture.

This was an extreme example, but it can be seen in so many everyday interactions men have with women they are attracted to, including co-workers, bar patrons, gym members, whatever, with the same results. Guys are too quick to smile and give praise (when it is not earned), whereas the woman really wants someone of at least equal (preferably higher) status, who is intriguing and under control (though at the same time positive and upbeat).

The likelihood of a successful interaction goes up when you talk to a woman as if you already know her, by adopting an easy-going, humorous attitude (I give examples in later sections).

You can still smile and telegraph some interest (after all, if you are completely aloof things won't progress), but interest can be built through playful teasing and the projection of confidence without shortchanging yourself.

In order to build attraction it is important to project respectable social status and value immediately. This can be accomplished by following the assignments in earlier chapters, on developing masculine body language and increasing your social and emotional intelligence by developing new hobbies and getting used to interacting with people.

For a woman to accept a date with you, a number of criteria must be met, the chief of which is attraction. Attraction can be built quickly if some (or preferably all) of these attributes are present:

- **Easy going confidence**
- **Intrigue**
- **Style**
- **Humor**

When you are not used to dealing with women it is all too easy to become nervous and make the same mistakes you have always made. Gathering up the courage to talk to a woman once or twice a year (or even once or twice a month) is not enough to help you shed your old habits. This is where Assignment #7 comes in. Get ready for action, because the ride starts now.

Assignment #7:

Approach 50 Women in 10 Days

This serves a dual purpose. It is a natural extension of previous assignments, but it concentrates on women. It may seem difficult at first, but let's be clear that *you are not expected to wow her with your charm for fifteen minutes.* Just go in and ask a question using one of your own or one of the examples given below.

This will plant the seed in your mind about the possibility of approaching women directly as a way to introduce yourself and carrying on a conversation with the intention of taking things further, so you don't need to rely exclusively on online dating sites.

This assignment need not be completed in consecutive days (after all, you are likely working or studying full-time), but it should be completed as soon as possible. Use the next four weekends, and a couple of weeknights. Even with a full-time job you should be able to complete this assignment in a single month. If it is stretched out to three or four months you won't get the full benefit.

This assignment will involve asking questions, some of which will more naturally lead to conversation than others. In the beginning ask the simple questions, then if you become more comfortable and desensitized to the process ask the more advanced questions.

Below are some examples, ranging from simple to more advanced. You may need to tailor them to the environment.

"Do you know the time?"

"Can you tell me if there is a coffee shop around here?"

"I need some caffeine, do you know of a good coffee shop around here?"

"How do you like that new [xyz] phone?"

"Hi, I'm buying a gift for my niece/nephew, do you think that iPod you're using would be too complicated for a ten year old?"

Even if the woman is not personally appealing to you, do not hesitate. Approach women who are slim, overweight, short, tall, older, etc. Do this in the same areas you used for Assignment #5. Each interaction will only last a few moments, which is fine at this stage. The last two examples are designed such that the woman may enter into conversation with you. You have the choice of either thanking her for her insight and then exiting, or continuing the conversation.

If you feel comfortable with continuing, remember that you can't talk about iPods all day. If you try to do so the conversation will naturally end after a couple of minutes. Again, there is nothing wrong with that at this early stage (Assignment #8 takes this to the next step), but if you would like to challenge yourself further now, you can redirect the subject by asking her what she's doing out and about. Is she shopping, on her way to work, on her way home from the gym (if she has a workout bag), etc.

If you don't feel comfortable with taking things further, just use the simple openers.

This assignment is a crash-course, rapid-fire method of getting you through the maximum number of approaches in as little time as possible, so you can become used to the process. Think of this as a total blitz of approaches, one after another. Keep an accurate tally of how many you make each day.

Do this even if you are tired and don't feel like going out. Some of your approaches will be weak because you are not in a good frame of mind. Others will be stellar in comparison, especially after you have already completed a few. This will give you terrific insight on how your frame of mind affects the interaction.

If the assignment seems daunting, think of it this way. *You are completing a work assignment in which you are required to get the opinion of fifty individuals, who just happen to be women.* Undoubtedly, some won't go as well as you hope, but this is to be expected, and it shouldn't be difficult because you are not expecting to get a date out of it – just a short statement. Would you expect all women you approach with a sales pitch for a new perfume to buy your product? No, but some may be interested.

This is an educational requirement for future interaction. As you finish speaking with one woman, think about going on to the next. After a while you won't have time to feel all that nervous, since you have a quota to fill. The more approaches you do, the less nervous you'll be.

Where to Engage with Women (Extended Duration)

There are countless scenarios where it is possible to interact with women. They range from random encounters when you are walking the street to structured social or educational events in which several people are together for extended periods, such as in a vacation tour group.

I list vacations and arts courses first because they are terrific ways to broaden your horizons, through which your general social skills will develop. Vacations can jump-start your social development, because while on holiday you are generally in a good mood, can forget about the stress you are under back home, and are more open to taking risks.

These are experiences that open up possibilities for interacting with women for an extended period. By "extended," I mean longer than a few minutes. Fleeting encounters, such as with women you meet while walking on a typical day will be covered later.

Vacations

Vacations are great for meeting people because you and just about everyone else who is on vacation let your defenses down and open up to new experiences and interactions. And since you are out of your home element (free of anyone you know), you are more likely to put yourself out there and interact with others.

Obviously, maintaining a long-term relationship with someone you met while on vacation is unlikely. The real value comes from the mindset you develop while away from home. Most people are friendlier, more outgoing, take social risks, laugh easier, and are generally more upbeat. If you haven't experienced this before, taking a vacation and then keeping up that positive mindset when you return home will be a terrific booster to your outlook and the way you interact with others.

Vacation experiences make for great conversation material back home, the delivery of which can be made even better by your enthusiasm as you relive the trip in your mind.

Guided Tour

A typical scenario for this is a group of 20 to 40 people travelling together on bus tour of a particular country or region, lasting anywhere from a day to a week (or even longer). In this type of tour the group stays together, travelling from one tourist spot to the next, stopping for lunch breaks, etc. Most people join the tour group alone, but occasionally there will be couples (or two friends) on vacation together.

Among the group, friendships and even relationships can start early, most coming to a natural end with the tour, but in some cases continuing afterward. It is not unheard of for a long-distance relationship to turn into a marriage, with one person moving to the other's location.

This is not guaranteed of course, so you shouldn't book your next vacation with the intent of hooking up or marrying someone on the trip. Just go and have fun, and enjoy the camaraderie, and bring your new upbeat attitude home with you.

Solo Vacation

Even if I'm not on a guided tour, I prefer travelling alone rather than with a friend from home because it forces me to be active and engage with people, instead of sticking with someone I already know. Meeting up with fellow travelers at the local attractions is easy. An organized walking tour of an attraction or district is a nice way to spend an afternoon, and it is great way to strike up a conversation with other people in the group. While in York, England, I went to dinner with some fellow travelers when the afternoon walking tour ended.

If you are staying at a hotel resort, outside tour options are usually available, but even if you choose to stay in the resort there are activities you can join that makes it easy to interact with others, especially if they are also travelling solo.

You can experience much the same effect without spending a lot of money or going far from home. Take a day off work and play tourist in your own (or nearby) city, visiting an area you don't go to often as long as there are some attractions and/or tours you can enjoy.

Special Interest Seminars

You don't need to go on an expensive vacation abroad to get the same effect closer to home. Most colleges offer specialized courses designed for people who wish to explore artistic pursuits, from home winemaking to stage acting, and range from a single afternoon to an entire work week. It may mean taking some vacation time off work, even though the course may be in your own city, but it is worth it.

I took a week-long comedy sketch writing course one summer. It was one of the best experiences of my life. I met many industry professionals and got to experience what a television comedy writer goes through, and had the opportunity to perform some of my own material on stage. Again, there is a bonding experience because you are working (having fun, really) with others to accomplish a goal.

More typically, most seminars are one or two days on the weekend, so you don't need to take time off work or school. They can be just as effective at giving you a fun opportunity to interact with people.

It is preferable to choose an arts or crafts subject or one with a theatrical theme, such as cooking, introductory acting or improv comedy – these get the entire class involved and there are many more chances to talk to those women in whom you may be interested.

Evening Hobby Courses

Earlier we talked about presentation and leadership courses to help with your public speaking, and courses designed to broaden your social circle. The courses suggested in this section are more for developing a new hobby, and as a bonus some can give credit towards a college certificate or diploma.

Think of these courses – anywhere from eight to twelve weeks – as something that contributes to your long-term growth first, and places to meet women second. This is a means to an end. Take the course with the intent of following through to learn a new skill, which can take you closer to your ultimate potential. Use some common sense when choosing a course. Taking an HTML coding class might make you marketable in a career sense, but there probably won't be many women attending, nor will it make you better at interacting with people.

Charitable Organizations

These organizations (e.g., community groups, environmental groups, churches, charities) are a great way to surround yourself with like-minded people. Having a common interest instantly gives you a connection and the chance to work with people that share your beliefs or interests. This can form the basis of new friendships or even a relationship.

Languages, Dancing, Acting

Learn a new language, or take acting or dancing lessons. There are usually more women than men present for all three of these pursuits.

Salsa dancing lessons are especially effective. Normally throughout the course you will be dancing with several different female classmates. No doubt some will be married or involved (or even taking lessons with a significant other), but odds are some will be single. If by some odd chance there are no single women, the course will be a terrific learning experience when it comes to interacting with the opposite sex. And finally, after several weeks of classes, when women you meet find out you can dance, well, you get the idea.

The thought of taking an acting course may be daunting. After all, you are up in front of an audience, which may be a real fear of yours. However, as with the presentation course discussed earlier, there are some mitigating factors. First, it is not the real you up on stage; you are playing the part of someone else, with lines that are not your own. Believe it or not, this makes a difference. You are under no pressure to discuss your life story. The words you say are those of a character in a play.

Second, most of the people in an introductory acting class will, like you, have had no acting experience. Some of them may be shy as well.

Like the other artistic pursuits, going over lines with your scene partners can be a bonding experience, and gives you a sense of purpose to do well in your class performance.

It is not necessary to take expensive acting courses from a prestigious school. Some community colleges offer continuing education acting programs with good instruction at reasonable prices.

Improv

I have put improvisation or improv in a separate category from acting, because of the added skills it can teach you. Improv classes are always great fun and provide many benefits, including social interaction and promoting the ability to think quickly. There is no homework, so even if you are extremely busy you can surely spare one night a week for the class.

At my local community college the theatrical program consisted of about seven courses in total, including Monologue, Scene Study, Improv, and a few more. I enjoyed improv the most, and ended up taking the advanced level at the college, and when those were exhausted I attended Second City Improv. Most medium to large cities have institutions with similar offerings.

There are many benefits to improv, beyond the immediate social interaction you get with classmates. It provides probably the most enjoyment you can have after a boring work day – many scenes you and your scene partners do in class end up being hilarious, intentionally or not. More important, the nature of the material and in-class exercises helps you think on your feet, which is invaluable when in conversation with women. Finally, the classes can expand on your sense of humor, and since women enjoy humor, this is something you can apply in conversations anywhere.

Most schools offer a series of courses from beginner to advanced, and most are reasonably priced. After reaching a certain level you are given the option of performing with your class in front of a live audience usually made up of friends and relatives of the class participants. Taking it further, if you have an aptitude you can join an advanced group that performs for larger, paying audiences.

When people find out that I have been involved in improv, they usually say they themselves could never do that. They view performing, especially without a script, as an almost impossible task. Having done it, I disagree.

Sure, there is the issue of performing in front of others, but if you stick to class workshops only, you can avoid this until (and if) you are ready to perform in front of a real audience. And the fact that everyone else in the class is inexperienced (just like you) means you are all coming up the ranks together, which takes a lot of the pressure off.

Additionally, there are a few rules to improv, the primary one being "Yes, and." What this means is, whatever your partner says, you agree with, and add to. Being up on stage with someone is a partnership, and you are there to help each other out.

As there are no physical props in improv you must mime or accept as fact the ideas your partner puts forth. The audience is part of the performance in the sense that they also accept the ideas. An example of a short improv scene might go like this:

James: "Hey Max, that's a real cool purple shirt you are wearing."
Max: "Yeah, and when I pull this string, it inflates! Watch this!"
(The performer playing Max pulls the imaginary string, while making a 'whooshing' sound. James reacts with amazement).
James: "Wow! That's just what we need to float to safety from the advancing herds of killer squirrels!"

The fact that Max accepted James' offer, and then built upon it with his own, allowed the story to progress. When the actors react with enthusiasm the performance is even more effective. Now look at a similar scene where the offer was not accepted:

James: "Hey Max, that's a real cool purple shirt you are wearing."
Max: "This isn't a purple shirt, it's a yellow vest."

Immediately the scene has lost energy due to blocking, and Max has left James holding the bag. James is forced to come up with something else, which may again be blocked by Max. You can see how this would not be a pleasant experience for James and the audience. Following some very basic rules greatly increases the chances of creating a successful scene, making things a lot easier for the performers.

As you've probably guessed by now, the above scenario can apply in real life conversations as well. I don't mean you need to agree with everything a person says, but by being enthusiastic, and building on their statements, you make a huge positive difference in your everyday conversations. Improv, just like conversation with a woman you've just met, is supposed to provide openings for the other person to join in and then provide openings for you too. It's a simple formula.

The only downside to improv classes is that unlike traditional acting there are usually more men enrolled than women. However, you can apply the lessons you learn in improv to your everyday interactions with people, especially women in whom you are interested. As you get to know each other, if you show an interest, ask questions, and add to what they are saying, your conversations will be far more rewarding. Apply the "yes, and" rule to your conversations.

For any artistic path, it goes without saying you must follow through. Don't go for a week or two and then quit because you feel uncomfortable. Keep at it through to the end. Don't miss any classes because you've convinced yourself you are too tired or not very good. They're excuses which feed your shyness. Before long you'll be glad you stuck with the classes.

That is one of the traps of being extremely reserved – you may take a leap of faith and actually join a course, but because you felt uncomfortable or nervous during the first class you may dread going back. You must push through that fear and keep going. As the weeks progress you will feel more and more comfortable, and then actually look forward to it.

Once the course ends, you will probably experience two opposing feelings: a sense of accomplishment, and a sense of relief that it is over. Don't let the relief part of the equation take over and prevent you from continuing. If you quit (or wait six months before taking another course), your progress will be lost. Keep your momentum up by taking the next level or even a different subject right away. Soon you will be looking forward to continuing with the next course.

Local activity clubs

Are you good at or do you want to learn rollerblading, mountain biking, hiking, etc.? Every major city has several activity clubs. Some offer many different activities to choose from, and some may have a 'singles' focus. Again, if you do not hit it off with any women attend anyway for the general social experience, and for the health and fitness benefits.

There may be some people in the group that you'll become friends with, and they may introduce you to people outside of the activity group, further expanding your social circle.

Gyms, Health Clubs

Getting yourself into decent physical condition can do wonders for your self esteem. But don't rely on home exercise equipment – these have a way of collecting dust, even if you had the best intentions when you purchased them. A gym membership is usually far more effective. The fact that you paid for the membership is a great motivator to use it, and getting out of the house, hopefully interacting with people, is a bonus.

Most gyms and fitness clubs offer an introductory training session with a paid membership. This session familiarizes you with the equipment, and the trainer will go over a few exercises to show proper technique. Further sessions are optional at extra cost and may be well worth it, especially in the early days.

The first couple of weeks will be rough, but if you stick with it you will like the results. Building core strength improves your posture and increases your energy level. Building muscle mass in your shoulders, back, chest, abdominals, and arms gives you a more defined look. You don't need to be ripped, but trimming a little excess fat and replacing it with muscle is always a good thing.

There may be a few single women at the gym. Most of them are there to keep fit rather than meet someone, but if you generate a friendly rapport who knows what could develop. Remember that nobody in the midst of a workout enjoys being interrupted.

The key to building rapport to a woman in a gym is to be friendly without telegraphing any romantic interest. At first you can smile and nod a greeting. When you see her the next time say *hello* to her directly. After that you can develop small talk about what exercises work best for each of you, preferred workout diets, health supplements, the heart monitor strap she's using, a difficult looking exercise she's doing that you're not, and a lot more subjects you'll think of on your own.

Do not be overly friendly and make a beeline towards her the moment she enters the workout area. Neither should you wear out your welcome by lingering too long while conversing (she's there to work out, after all). You should be treating her like a person, not a woman you want to sleep with (she will likely have had other men hitting on her, so her guard will be up). As time goes on the possibility exists for a mutual romantic attraction to develop.

Online Dating

When internet dating first came on the scene in the mid-nineties some people attached a stigma to it: *You met online? Couldn't you meet somebody the "real" way?* The "real" way supposedly meant bars, or any other place people gather, or through a friend.

That stigma has long since vanished, and for many people online dating has now become the number one way to meet a potential partner. That's not to discount traditional avenues; people still date coworkers, those they meet at parties, or through blind dates set up by friends. However, with its popularity the web has broadened the possibilities of finding a partner.

Telephone dating services have been around longer than the web versions, and have hung on as a niche alternative despite the explosive growth of web-based dating sites. Some have affiliations with or are owned by web-based services.

Internet-based

Internet dating sites have the advantage of letting the member upload one or more photos to go with their profile, so you immediately know what they look like, provided the person uploads a decent photo. Some people upload travel photos that are more about the scenery than the person, making you squint to obtain any detail. Or, they upload a group photo in which you're supposed to pick them out in a sea of fifteen faces.

Some members only include a sentence or two in their description; I prefer they have at least a paragraph of their goals and aspirations, as this can give the reader some insight into their personality, and hint at whether the two of you are compatible.

Most major dating sites contain thousands of profiles, especially if you live in a large city. And while this is great for giving you lots of choice, it can also be a detriment. With so many profiles to choose from, many people only respond to those they find outstandingly attractive. The trouble is, many others are doing the same, so there is a lot of competition among the most physically attractive users.

This also means we might forgo contact with those that might otherwise be terrific people. I have been guilty of this in the past; regretfully, I have likely ignored some very datable 'sevens' because I was on the lookout for 'eights' and 'nines,' and I'm sure that is also true of some women who viewed my profile. Why would they initiate contact with me if the photo of the next guy is 10% more appealing than mine?

It's unfortunate so many of us take the attitude that someone better is just around the corner. It can mean months (even years) wasted and many opportunities lost. Nowadays people are fixated on finding the perfect mate, one that meets a long list of compatibility and attractiveness requirements. Despite this, even if a person finds 'the one,' divorce rates remain sky high, so once again the almost unlimited choice does not make it easier to find a compatible partner.

Telephone-based

Phone-based dating is similar to web-based in that the user browses through dating profiles, though instead of viewing a photograph and reading a description, they listen to the person's recorded voice profile. This has the advantage of giving you a better handle on the person's intelligence, personality, and demeanor, which in most cases comes across more readily than in a written profile. This is the likely reason for its enduring popularity with some daters (even among young, net-savvy individuals) despite its use of old, voice-only phone technology.

The disadvantage is the lack of visual representation of the person, though some phone services have a simple web site that gives members the option to upload photos, which is indicated in their voice profile summary, so those browsing the profile can log in to view a photo. If you persevere and listen to many profiles you can usually find some that are appealing. Although I had many false starts with phone dating, one woman stood out from the rest.

Though I went into this looking for a relationship, the previous night she steered the conversation towards sex. Women have sexual needs too; that she was intelligent and articulate only made the conversation better.

Her fantasy was to meet a guy she'd never seen before and immediately take him to a nearby lingerie shop, into the change room, whereupon she would strip and change into a new bra and panties. I wasn't about to pass this up or give her a stern lecture on morality, so we agreed to meet at an upscale downtown mall, in the bookstore. On the phone she said she was attractive, but having been burned so many times in the past I wasn't expecting much; people often exaggerate their looks, it's human nature. What if she was like the last girl I met off the phone for coffee?

My experience a month before was almost enough to make me quit the whole phone-dating thing. Not that she was an awful person, but she had lied about her appearance. Women say guys lie about their height, but this woman had completely misled me about her weight, being about 75 pounds heavier than she claimed. Call me superficial, but there has to be some physical attraction, and I had none for her.

So this day at the mall I had my guard up. I didn't see her at the appointed time so occupied myself browsing books. But a few minutes later there she was, just as she had described herself: a tall, slim, curvy redhead with sultry eyes and a nice smile.

We introduced ourselves and made small talk for a minute, but she wanted to get right to it (who was I to argue?) and led me arm-in-arm out the bookstore and towards the nearby lingerie shop.

We browsed the shop's offerings and she picked out a skimpy panty and bra set, then asked the female clerk if she minded if her boyfriend went into the change room with her. The clerk said it was fine, so we entered a change booth and shut the door.

I sat on the bench. She looked at me and smiled, then started to undress. Part of me couldn't believe this was happening, and I half-expected her to change her mind. But she didn't hesitate, and within seconds was completely nude.

At that point the clerk knocked on the door asking if everything was all right. We replied in the affirmative and my date put her clothes back on. She paid for the lingerie and we spent some time together.

Disclaimer: my experience with this audacious woman was a pleasant diversion. Encounters such as this are unusual, and not to be expected (or even encouraged, given the risk; if a sexual encounter is possible bring a condom and practice safe sex, or pass).

But much of this book is about numbers and pushing your personal boundaries. Getting out of the house more frequently; increasing the number of people you meet in a week; ramping up your social contacts; starting new hobbies and courses, so that your calendar is filled; meeting and talking to more women (and feeling at ease when doing so); and of course, increasing the number of dates you go on.

Sooner or later, the pieces will fall into place.

Don't initiate sex talk

Despite the events leading up to the previous story's conclusion, it is not a good idea for you to engage in sex talk with a woman, whether it's by email, texting, Facebook, or over the phone, unless she does so first. Doing so may make you appear vulgar in her eyes, even if she has been acting flirty or suggestive in her communications thus far. Overt sexual communication can be returned, but let her do the escalating. Match, but do not surpass the level she sets.

Tips for Constructing a Winning Profile

There are things you can do to make your profile as appealing as possible, the most important of which is to have an upbeat, detailed description of yourself. Just as with my earlier recommendation on posting on enthusiast sites, for written profiles avoid using short forms for words (e.g., "ur" instead of "your") - littering your online profile with "texting" words will make you seem lazy and unintelligent. Also avoid pointless catchphrases like starting your profile with "Wazup?"

One thing that bothers me in women's profiles is that oft-repeated phrase, "I feel just as comfortable in evening wear as jeans and a t-shirt, and so should you." Can we try for some originality, please? Stay away from clichés such as this.

Try to upload a clear, recent photo of yourself. If you don't have one ask a friend to take a few, preferably outside on an overcast day (too much sun can make a photo harsh; cloudy days make for better photographs). Avoid taking a mobile phone photo in front of the bathroom mirror; this comes off as a bit tawdry and cheap. Also avoid appearing shirtless or wearing sunglasses; women want to see your eyes, and most want you to convey a little class, which going shirtless does not, no matter how good you think you look.

Have several photos in different situations: one from a wedding you attended (so you are dressed up), one with a group of friends (to show you are social, though not one of you chugging a beer!), something casual, and something sporting. Have head shots as well as body shots.

Spend some time describing your positive attributes, your hobbies, goals for the future, and what you hope to find in a partner. Seriously, spend some time at this. The more detailed you are, the better. Women are more likely than men to actually read a profile in its entirety.

This may seem obvious, but many guys are guilty of this faux pas: do not upload or send nude photos of yourself, unless you are on an Adult/XXX site where people expect it. On regular dating sites, women are put-off by what they term as vulgar shots, and generally will not reply to any guy that sends them such a photo.

Your profile name and title should stand out, and convey mystery and masculinity. And as with almost all social interactions, using humor can enhance your profile.

Interestingly, you can also use humor to weed out humorless individuals. For example, in my online profile under the category "What I like to do on a first date" I wrote: "After we have a coffee, I may recruit you for a non-violent crime spree." Most women found this funny, but a few wrote to ask if I was joking or not.

Your Facebook page can also act as a potential gateway to romance with female acquaintances (or friends of friends on Facebook). The same rules apply for keeping your profile upbeat and having a variety of photos.

Speed Dating

Speed dating has become popular in the last few years, and is touted as a way for the busy professional to meet a potential partner. Some speed dating events only use age as a criteria for attending (so the attendees are roughly in the same age group), while others are more definitive, targeting university graduates or even specific religions or ethnic groups.

The basic premise is to have about a dozen men and a dozen women in a reserved area of a lounge or upscale restaurant. The women are always seated at a table, while the men rotate from one table to another, in sequential order, speaking to each woman in turn for about ten minutes. At the ten minute mark the hostess bangs a gong to indicate it is time to rotate to the next woman. Both male and female participants have cards on which to write the name of each person they speak with, along with a *Yes* or *No* checkmark. At the end of the evening, the cards are returned to the hostess, who compiles the results of the card checkmarks. Should one or both people say *No*, there is no matchup. Should both say *Yes*, the hostess sends an email with mutual contact information.

Speed dating looks interesting on paper, but there are several problems with it. First, while it may be possible to mingle for a time before or after the event, during the event itself you are only given ten minutes to converse with each 'date,' so if you are the type of person that needs warm up time to get your nerves under control, you may not be presenting your best self in that ten minutes. Also, the one or two most attractive or charismatic members of each gender attending tend to get the most hits on the scorecards, perhaps to the exclusion of most of the other attendees. Finally, as with any random group of a dozen people, the odds of any of them being what you judge as attractive is fairly low.

However, I suggest you try speed dating because it can be excellent practice for your interaction with women. Don't go in thinking you must perform well or hope of finding a girlfriend. Go in for the conversation and body language practice it will offer you. Try changing your body language and tonality from one woman to the next, and see how they react.

Six

PICKUP ARTISTS

Courtship is a complex social behavior that very few guys are naturally good at, and since there are so many stages to the process it's no surprise men fail, even some of those that aren't particularly shy. You need to make an approach (online or in person), get through the telephone stage, proceed to the first in-person date, and then be subject to her post-date evaluation. And of course within each stage there are progressive steps in which you are required to build interest and attraction. You need to be at least competent at every stage for there to be a second date (or even a first date).

Since courtship behaviors are mostly learned, if you are struggling it makes sense to seek help from those that might be more knowledgeable. There are books and seminars on how to make you more presentable and marketable in the job world, so why would there not be similar offerings for men who need help with dating?

In Assignment #7 we discussed talking to women who have attracted your interest. I gave a few example openers and discussed adding humor to the interaction. Now that we are actually talking to women and engaging them in conversation, it is worth going into the realm of the Pickup Artist, and discussing things they might be able to teach us.

The Pickup Artist (PUA) has gained a lot of notoriety in the last few years, largely due to their heavy presence on the internet, through high-profile interviews on talk shows, and in bestselling books such as *The*

Game: Penetrating the Secret Society of Pickup Artists. There's a lot of PUA jargon, so bear with me here.

Many critics dismiss PUAs as charlatans preaching false hope to Average Frustrated Chumps (AFCs). They point out that some of the techniques promoted are questionable at best and unethical at worst, such as tossing veiled insulting remarks (Negs) towards attractive women (thus increasing your value, or rather, reducing her value from her own perspective), employing Neuro-Linguistic Programming techniques (NLP – suggestive or leading words) to subliminally boost your attractiveness, and Peacocking (wearing outrageous or unusual clothing or accessories) to make yourself stand out.

These techniques along with approach and conversational skills are designed to get results ranging from a number close (getting her contact information, ideally a phone number), a kiss close (ideally a make out session), or even a same night lay (SNL, where you take her back to her place or yours).

If you are suspicious of the concepts, know that not all PUAs should be lumped into a single group, and these negative connotations don't give a full account of the community. Just as there are various forms of meditation techniques or martial arts, there are different schools of thought in the seduction community. For example, some are a little more forward thinking and recommend you use their techniques to help in your quest for a monogamous relationship.

Fortunately, the days of cheesy pickup lines are gone (if they ever really existed). Most techniques today involve the adoption of new self-positive attitudes and conversational skills designed to make you more desirable to women.

PUAs have their own subculture, and as you can see from above, acronyms for describing situations and methods. And while I'm an advocate of the value some PUA teachings can bring to the table, there are so many PUA 'gurus' out there these days that it pays to do some research before handing over any cash for their programs. Some rely more on polishing your lines rather than improving your self-confidence, and some of their web sites read like a bad R-rated infomercial: *"Have any woman dripping with desire within ten minutes of meeting you!"*

The Game by Neil Strauss is an interesting book because it describes the author's descent into the PUA subculture, and does not hold back when it comes to revealing the rewards and pitfalls of the lifestyle. Strauss describes how he was able to attain huge successes with women by practicing PUA material he had learned from various mentors, and goes on to say it became an empty existence on some levels, but one that he was able to come to terms with in the end. While he is still in the business, in his book Strauss concludes his journey by espousing respect for others as one of the keys to success, something that some pickup artists ignore.

Many of the central personalities in *The Game* have their own following (Ross Jeffries, Mystery, and others), along with Strauss himself. Much of what these guys preach makes perfect sense; most of them hold personal grooming, style, and presentation as central to their success.

And from reading about their exploits we see that they do get results, using techniques that are field tested and refined on random female subjects in night clubs, restaurants, and even on the street. However, while some of them are very good at getting phone numbers from women, what struck me as odd for many was their lack of success in getting, and keeping, a long term relationship.

Neil himself was successful at getting a girlfriend towards the end of his book, but most of the others, including Tyler Durden, Papa (all pseudonyms; most PUAs go by nicknames) failed to get anything much beyond a number and a kiss. Mystery, Neil's primary mentor, had some trouble maintaining relationships (at least as portrayed in the book), though he and Neil managed some impressive one night stands with women. Many of the other PUAs could not even manage that. Most of their success was measured in how many numbers each of them had by the end of the night.

While I admire some of their opening techniques, that is not success. The vast majority of Pick Up Artists profiled in *The Game* could not translate their awesome approach skills into anything meaningful, even if they could get a date. This tells me that some of them have incomplete or superficial skills. They can break the ice with magic tricks, storytelling anecdotes, and even a kiss, but they lack the depth to even start a relationship, much less maintain one.

I don't want to give the impression that they have nothing to teach. Strauss' book focused mostly on a large group of people that were living in a mansion rented by Neil, Mystery and a rotating group of followers (some of whom became competitors), and all of the ensuing politics and rivalries that resulted. Some of the students ended up splitting off into groups that started holding their own classes with new students, and one gets the idea that most of them started teaching well before they were ready.

That being said, many of the established PUA outfits you see on the web have real skills to offer, and the online PUA community is great for positive support, giving pointers on where to meet women, calming your approach anxiety, and how to keep a conversation going. However some of them fall down by concentrating on routines rather than convincing guys to develop their inner self.

As long as you remember that you must have substance to go with the sizzle, PUA teachings can be valuable. In fact, some organizations offer in-field training (boot camps) that give you real-world instruction on approaching women and building attraction through conversation and body language.

Below is a brief overview some of the most famous PUAs in the online world at present (there are many additional practitioners of course):

Ross Jeffries

Considered one of the founding fathers of the PUA movement, Jeffries uses suggestive words, gestures and body language to subliminally lead a woman into being attracted to you. It is all a little more substantive than that of course, but Jeffries practices the art of suggestion and persuasion to build attraction.

I have mixed feelings about this method. It is not unethical to sell yourself; salespeople do it all the time, trying to convince you their product is better than the rest. What they are saying is not necessarily untrue. They may just be leaving out the disadvantages or weaknesses. All of us do that on a regular basis. Would you deliberately tell a job interviewer anything truly negative about yourself? The problem is relying on the technique too much. Without bettering yourself as a person, the technique can ring hollow. And Jeffries goes quite far in his claims.

Jeffries pushes literally dozens of products on his web site, but one thing he said that I admire was his admission that if you have a whole collection of PUA instructional material and are still having difficulty with women the solution is not to buy more material. You must examine what you are doing wrong. To that, I would add you need to work on your confidence and social skills, bettering yourself in all areas of your life. Once you do this, the rest flows naturally.

If Jeffries' method appeals to you, I recommend you first buy a book on NLP to gain some knowledge of the foundation of his programs.

Mystery (Erik von Markovik)

Equally famous (and arguably more widely emulated in the PUA community than Jeffries) is Mystery. This is the guy that touts Peacocking theory (wearing outrageous accessories to stand out), the three second-rule (approaching a woman within three seconds of spotting her so you don't lose your nerve), magic tricks (to draw people in), Negs (to show you are not impressed by beauty, which throws some women off balance), escalating emotions to build attraction, and then feigning disinterest (so she will have to work to get back your attention).

In his first book *The Mystery Method: How to Get Beautiful Women Into Bed* Mystery is open to making approaches anywhere, but in his follow up offering *The Pickup Artist: The New and Improved Art of Seduction* he advocates dance clubs as the number one place to attract women, because of the sheer number of beautiful bodies in these places, and the emotional release when there is dancing and drinking. That logic is sound, but he assumes everyone is comfortable in dance clubs.

It's difficult for me to relate to Mystery's second book because of his de-emphasis of every location but clubs, and the fact that he's so flamboyant with the peacocking. It works for him, but it's generally not for me. Still, his approach skills are unquestioned, and he has a lot to teach about building attraction through assertive and confident behavior.

Though it has been available for a few years now in this rapidly evolving field, his debut book *The Mystery Method* is still a good seller because it has some excellent foundation information, if being a little hard to follow at times with all the theory he discusses. Mystery is the founder of Venusian Arts, an online company that markets his material.

Neil Strauss (aka Style)

Author of *The Game: Penetrating the Secret Society of Pickup Artists* Strauss was Mystery's student and eventually rose to match (or even surpass) his teacher. It is fascinating to read Strauss's evolution from an AFC to full-fledged PUA, and his progress is inspiring. Unlike Mystery, he does not rely on magic tricks, but he does practice Negs and disinterest, balanced with humor. He also injects a lot of teasing and storytelling in his interactions, all of which can be used to build attraction.

Of all the famous PUAs, Strauss is one of the more well rounded, partly because he studied under so many mentors (including Ross Jeffries). Unlike some of the others he does spend some time discussing grooming, being sociable with people (outside of pickup), and bettering yourself en route to becoming a PUA. But as with Mystery, I find there is a little too much emphasis on Negs, and I don't think Neil is any better than the average guy at keeping a relationship going.

By the end of his book, Neil gives the impression he is ready to turn his back on some of the more subversive PUA techniques, and in some of his later material touts self-confidence and lifestyle as better motivators to success with women. Neil has partnered up with several other PUAs to create a seduction educational system called the Stylelife Academy, which also hosts a useful online forum anyone can join.

Michael Marks

Marks takes much of what Mystery and Neil Strauss offer but without the emphasis on Negs. Though he does advocate playful teasing to build rapport, and dressing with unusual accessories so you'll stand out, he emphasizes inner game and masculine behavior as the primary motivators to success.

Though all PUAs teach that men should never be submissive in any interaction, more than most Marks is cognizant of the masculine-feminine difference and how women want the man to dominate interactions. This entails leading the frame, talking and acting in a calm, in-control yet playful manner, and being mindful of when it is time to escalate and build sexual attraction.

Like Strauss, Marks emphasizes building your self-worth, including building your social circle but he takes it a step further by advocating that you develop a proactive approach to life by adopting an interesting new lifestyle, and maintaining a physical training regimen to stay in shape, believing that by being in good physical condition you will also be in good mental and emotional health.

It should be pointed out that PUA techniques are constantly evolving with most practitioners moving towards the inner confidence method, and Marks has been ahead of the curve in this regard.

Marks has produced an excellent eBook and an audio CD set that has some great insight into mental game and approach techniques.

Nick Savoy

Savoy, along with Mystery, founded the Mystery Method, but after Mystery left to form his own company, Savoy changed the company name to Love Systems and recruited other PUAs to help refine the curriculum.

Love Systems is a big promoter of seminars and live-in-the-field instruction. The company employs proven theories while at the same time keeping the material current with refinements and periodic updates.

Some of the PUAs in Love Systems (including such names as Cajun and Tenmagnet, among others) have been featured on television programs or news articles. Each individual under the Love Systems banner brings his own style to the mix, a great advantage if after reading their biographies on the site you find one that focuses on areas that match what you need to work on (club approaches, group approaches, etc.).

Like most of the others, Love Systems has a useful online support group that you can join to ask questions and read about field reports, tips and programs.

PUA Offerings

These and other PUAs offer a variety of training material, including books (eBooks or print), audio CDs, DVDs, live classroom seminars, and individual coaching by phone or in person. Costs go up with the level of personal interaction, with classroom seminars costing $500 to $1,000, and in-field coaching $2,000-$3,000.

Study the Pick Up Artist materials selectively, and understand that if you suffer from extreme shyness they are not quick-fixes to what ails you (e.g., if you are terrified at the prospect of talking to strangers you must work on that fear before jumping into a PUA seminar – another reason why my assignments in this book are so important). All of the individuals I've cited are legitimate and have put a lot of work into course material, drawing from personal experience and from collaboration with other PUAs.

When looking at PUA material it helps to familiarize yourself with the language used in the community. In addition to the examples above, here are a few more common terms.

Wing – your prospecting partner. If you go out to a bar or club it is more effective to go with a buddy than go out alone. Wings help by making each other appear sociable, praising each other in front of women, playing off the other by filling in conversation gaps or adding interesting stories, and occupying the group so the other can spend time conversing with the woman he is interested in.

Set – the number and gender of those you are approaching. A *mixed set* includes both males and females, so when you approach you will need to find out the relationship status of the individuals in the group. For example, are the guys friends or relatives of the woman you are interested in, or is she in a relationship with one of them? The easiest way to do this after your opener is to ask "so, how do you guys know each other?" A *two-set* is composed of two women; a *three-set* composed of three women, and so on.

Target – the woman you are interested in, usually part of a set. When approaching a group, if you direct most of your attention to the target she will sense your interest early and become self conscious, putting up a barrier. Additionally, it is rude to ignore her friends. The solution is to give the other women an equal amount of attention (or even a little more) to win over her friends to show you are a good guy. Later in the interaction you can direct more of your time to the target. Having a wing is ideal in this situation because he can then keep the friends occupied while you build rapport with the woman you are interested in.

Push-pull – if you are in a conversation with a woman and she begins to show interest, theoretically you can increase the attraction if you aren't completely enamored by her. In other words, you can smile and praise her (e.g., "I like that you travel, it means you are aware of what's going on in the world"), then turn away for a moment and say a word or two to your friend. Then go back to the woman with further conversation. This can also be physical (if she hints that she is comfortable with touching). Reach down and give her wrist a light underhand squeeze, while your shoulders are facing her, then turn your body outward so your shoulders are perpendicular to her body while you take a sip of your drink and look at the rest of the bar. Then after a moment return your focus to the woman. This is advanced technique, and it assumes you are comfortable with approaches and conversation.

So What Works?

Now that we've had a brief overview of Pickup Artists, what direction should you go? You could spend a ton of money, buying products from each of them, employ their various methods, and try to pinpoint what works best. I'm not necessarily knocking that angle, but it can get expensive and overwhelming.

Having been aware of the PUA community for several years, I have noticed some interesting trends. Pick-up is part behavioral science and part art, and like any group or movement it evolves as techniques come in and out of favor. Some of the original players stick to their tried and true methods, others change as they see new trends emerge, and some rival groups even partner up for a time to market special packages, then split off again to do their own thing.

The latest trends have some PUAs moving away from the Negs and magic tricks, while putting more emphasis on natural conversation skills – a welcome change. Some of the old guard continues to tout the same methods they have always offered, but most regularly update their material with new formulas designed to keep themselves on the cutting edge of the art form.

Some people are uncomfortable with the concept of Pickup Artists, believing that any man who studies such material is only looking for one night stands. For some men this may be true, but other practitioners have honorable motives, simply looking for assistance in their quest to find a fulfilling relationship. Many women have no idea of how difficult it is for a reserved man to approach her and ask her out. If studying attraction material teaches those men who struggle how to gain confidence in their interactions with women, it is a viable, legitimate route to follow.

I believe doing your best to be a well-rounded individual, developing new hobbies and interests, working on your social skills through interactions with people (e.g., taking classes, and the opportunity to engage in conversation whenever possible), and developing a confident, care-free attitude (removing limiting thoughts and behaviors) are the necessary first steps. This will help you develop a rock-solid foundation on which you can continue to build and refine your persona. Once you have made those changes in your life, you will possess the four qualities that women find most attractive in a person:

- **Easy going confidence**
- **Intrigue**
- **Style**
- **Humor**

Those are the four magic attributes you need to attract women. In fact, if you are outstandingly good at any two of the above that may be enough! However, if it were as easy as understanding those words none of us would need help in getting a date. Repeating the exercises in this book will allow you to get there. You may also benefit from studying PUA material. Just be selective and don't go crazy with your credit card.

Seven

PUTTING THEORIES into PRACTICE

The rest of this book deals with the actual practice of making approaches, along with tips on dealing with mental roadblocks and approach anxiety. But first here is a relevant example on self-help and taking initiative.

A few years ago while between jobs I attended a seminar on a subject that piqued my interest. An author was promoting his book on freelance business writing, the topic being *"how to make a full time living writing for large and small businesses in six months or less."*

The gist of the seminar was, if you were a reasonably good writer and had some people skills, you could tap the corporate world's demand for good copywriting, be it for advertisements, brochures, annual reports, etc. The author was very convincing, making a sound case for something that seemed right up my alley. After the seminar I purchased his how-to book and, using the suggestions within its pages, resolved to call local advertising firms, graphic design houses, and web masters to see if they could use a freelance writer.

Since the presenter was very sincere and effective in getting his ideas across, I figured many of the other sixty-odd people at the seminar would also be calling the same firms. Over the next six weeks, using the Yellow Pages I made it my full-time job to call every one of those business categories in the city, and then some. I made an average of 50 calls per day, and at the end of several weeks had made over 1100 phone calls, some of which led to paid assignments.

Let's be clear – despite still being a very reserved person, I was cold calling, phoning up businesses, large and small, and asking to speak with the proprietor, marketing manager, or whomever else would be in charge of farming out writing assignments. None of these people had ever heard of me; I was just some guy offering a service. This is what it sometimes takes to succeed in the business world, to get out and do something outside of your comfort zone. Most people are reluctant to cold call because they think the person is too busy to hear your sales pitch or already has someone doing the job.

You might think most of them would give me a quick "thanks but no thanks" and then hang up. But for over half of the people I spoke with that wasn't the case.

Most of those I called were very receptive to using a freelance writer, or at least keeping the name of a writer on file should the need arise. And while a few had used freelancers in the past, not one of them indicated they had recently fielded a similar call from another writer. In other words, it didn't look like any of the other people that attended the seminar were calling up businesses like I was. That was too bad for them, because I picked up some good clients and made thousands of dollars in extra income. My six-week cold-calling effort (and periodic follow-up over the next year) paid off.

One of my fears going in was of the competition; but apparently, nobody else from the seminar was doing much calling. This was an eye-opener for me. Most people fail right out of the gate, because they don't even try. Even though they may attend a self-help seminar with the best intent, they won't put in the effort necessary to succeed, either because they are too timid, too frightened of leaving their comfort zone, or because they simply lack the will power.

And of course the parallel here is that if you are to take a new direction in life, including developing your social and dating skills, you need to put in the time and effort. There are many women out there who would be more than willing to be approached for conversation and a date. Making approaches is another way of cold calling, and it's a proven method that works.

Where to Engage with Women (Fleeting Duration)

These are the types of encounters that are the most interesting, exciting, and frustrating. How many times have you encountered a woman you find attractive on the street or in the bookstore, only to look on helplessly as she passes by, gone forever? You dream of the possibilities, what you might have done to open a conversation, but it is all for naught. And the situation repeats itself, time and again. The solution is to develop your cold approach and conversational skills. The key to any good approach is:

- Open strongly, ideally with humor
- Smile and be upbeat
- Listen to her response and build on it by showing interest (lessons learned in improv)

Making Approaches

There are many ways to meet women, including through:

- Blind dates set up by friends
- Work relationships that turn romantic
- Online or telephone dating
- Trips and vacations
- Random encounters in shops, the street, in malls or on public transit

All of these are potential dating areas but the last one – random encounters with women you meet while out on errands or going about your daily business – demand the most skill. Much of what follows deals with developing this skill, but the techniques learned can be applied to any method you use to meet and converse with women (such as being introduced by friends).

If you are extremely well-built and good looking, women will notice and send you signals they are interested. Occasionally some may even approach you directly for conversation. But even if you are such a fortunate individual, it is still up to you to read the signals and act on them. In addition, you must be able to present yourself in the ways described above, with confidence. The good-looking guy will fail if he demonstrates self-conscious or needy behavior (yes, some good-looking guys are insecure). Women will notice a lack of confidence within the first few seconds of an interaction and eliminate him as a prospect.

There is good news for all the less-than-great-looking guys out there. If you are confident and secure in yourself, you will have far more success than the good-looking guy who is insecure. Don't confuse confidence with arrogance. If you walk around trying to express a tough, *don't mess with me* aura, you will only be portraying yourself as intimidating and unapproachable and an insecure individual. Instead, be the unflappable guy that is unaffected by other's behavior.

Despite all the talk of equality in modern society, when it comes to dating It is usually up to you as the man to take the initiative. Under most circumstances women will rarely, if ever, come to you, asking you out. They are not going to knock on your door asking you why you haven't talked to them. Approaching women for conversation and a date is a daunting prospect for most men, but you will succeed if you are able to talk to women as if you already know them and are able to build rapport and attraction.

Approach means different things to different people. If your goal is to be more comfortable at gatherings and socializing with people and women you meet through friends, while on vacation, or through everyday interactions, the assignments are designed to address this.

However, I would recommend taking it to the next level. If you set about this with the intention of developing the skill to approach women out of the blue (i.e., on the street), you will be taking your skills to the absolute pinnacle.

Why Approach Women when I can do Online Dating?

If you follow the advice given up to now, you will likely expand your social circle, make some new friends, and will have developed your conversational skills through practice. This (along with any online dating you may be doing) will not only increase the number of women you encounter, but also increase the chances of having a successful interaction leading to a date.

However, you may be hoping for more. Perhaps the majority of new women you are meeting at parties are married or involved. Maybe the women that message you online don't appeal to you because they are outside of your age range.

Internet dating is a legitimate, viable method for connecting with women. But some guys don't have much success, for a number of reasons, even if you construct what most people would consider a winning profile:

- **You may not be photogenic**
- **You may have trouble expressing yourself in the written word**
- **You may be deemed too old by the women you are interested in**

These difficulties can largely be overcome in person. For example, if you are able to project a confident, upbeat personality, women that might have found you to be plain or too old when viewing your online profile will be far less likely to have such feelings when seeing you in person.

Some guys can be charming via e-mail, but the real challenge is maintaining that charisma in person. If you are constantly blowing dates and find it difficult to get a second (or third) date, you will likely benefit from the practice of approaching women directly.

But to answer the question – why bother making approaches to women when the internet is so convenient? The answer is, power and choice. The power to approach women in any situation gives you the ability to go after women you find attractive.

If you develop the talent to approach women in public, or the ability to be charismatic during conversations at a social gathering, you will broaden your choices exponentially. Who among us has not been disappointed with the bulk of women that message us on dating sites? Wouldn't it be better to date a woman that appeals to you in person, like that attractive graduate student in the bookstore? You bet it would.

Talk to Women as If You Already Know Them

While in a bookstore in the greeting cards section, I picked up a funny hologram card with a cat on the cover, whose facial expression changed depending on the angle at which you viewed the card. I laughed aloud when I saw the effect, and turned to the woman standing near me (one I had noticed just before) and said, "Hey, check this out," holding the card out to her while moving it slightly so she could see the effect.

She laughed and said it was cool. We then talked about buying cards for Mother's Day. It was very relaxed because it was a little quip given in a familiar manner, as if she were a friend. This always has a disarming effect (especially when done with humor), putting the woman at ease.

Going in with confidence and displaying the ability to talk to women as if you already know them will make it easier to shift into rapport and attraction. This entails speaking and asking questions in a way that you do with your friends. This creates a level of comfort, the exact opposite result from the usual stilted, safe conversation that most guys use.

For the first few minutes of an interaction, do not ask the same tired old questions such as what she does for a living and where she lives. Instead, make observations about the surroundings or her great style of dress. Moderate, truthful compliments work well, but excessive or artificial compliments can arouse suspicion.

Observational humor can make things so much easier than a standard opener like *Hi, my name is Mike,* and then trying to carry on from there. The former is interesting and works well in a setting where people are not mingling; the latter is better at a social gathering like a party.

If you are in a bookstore, you need not be in the card section to find something amusing. You can also use book titles. Scan the titles in the aisle and find an unusual or bad title. Then pull out the book and say to the woman standing next to you, *Really, would you buy a book with this title? I think they dropped the ball on this one!* Smile as you show her the book, and then make a comment on how many uninteresting books you must sift through before you find a good one, and then transition from there, into conversation, asking what books she finds interesting.

What if her boyfriend is lurking around the corner?

Even though I only approach women that are not wearing an engagement or wedding ring, there is always the chance they have a boyfriend. And if you are in a shopping venue like a bookstore, he could be lurking a couple of aisles over.

This is one contributing fear that guys have about approaching a woman: the fear that if she happens to have a boyfriend, she'll call the brute over to dispatch you. This is a misconception – the only time it might turn dangerous is if you wander into some biker bar and start in on the club leader's woman.

First, it is not at all obvious that you are hitting on her – at this point you're only making pleasant, interesting conversation. Second, most women are not offended that you are talking to them. Quite the opposite; most are flattered.

And third, the lurking boyfriend doesn't occur all that often and I only mention it to make you aware of possibility, and that it is easy to disengage smoothly – simply say it was nice talking to her, and walk away. No harm no foul – move on to the next location and the next target.

But when you get really comfortable with approaches, in a club setting you can converse with the boyfriend as well. It pays to get really good at the skill of working the group, allowing you to approach mixed groups, befriend them, and within a few minutes find out who among the women are single.

Approach Often to Build Confidence

If all you do say during a cold approach is, *Hi, you have a great sense of style, would you like to go for a coffee?* you won't have a high success rate. Still, approaching a high number of women without any expectation is a great exercise in confidence building.

This is a good strategy to follow in the beginning (as described in Assignment #7). Keep the first few interactions sincere but short, only following up with further conversation if you are comfortable. Later as you lose your approach anxiety you can work on extending the interaction to build rapport.

Warm Up Before Making Approaches

Pick up may be an art, but it also helps to think of it as a sport – one of mind, body and emotion. Choose any sport you are good at, be it golf, tennis, basketball, skiing, or anything else. All of these sports have challenges. In golf, you may need to hit the ball between two bunkers, which may require a very straight drive. In tennis, you may be playing against someone that has a terrific net game. In basketball you may have an opposing player that is on you like glue, preventing you from receiving a pass. In skiing, you may be in a slalom race on an icy course with low visibility.

All of the above are challenging conditions. All require some degree of mental and physical preparation. You may need to concentrate on your breathing, stance, balance, reaction time, while keeping yourself focused. If you approach the task half-heartedly, or while distracted or in a bad mood, you will most likely fail.

You can maximize your chances for a successful approach by warming up, just like in your favorite sport. If you resolve to make four approaches in one day, the first one or two will have a higher chance of failure if you just go in cold, hoping you will get lucky. If you do this, you will most likely forget some of the more basic rules, and will have less success. Do not rely on luck. As you know with sports, luck takes a back seat to being prepared. Before your first approach of the day:

1) Take a deep breath and exhale slowly.
2) Think of something positive that will get you in a good mood, like an excellent goal you got during the game with your friends on the weekend, or how you felt after being promoted at work, etc.
3) Smile to yourself (even if you can't think of something positive or funny) – this will help get you into a positive mindset.
4) Straighten up your posture; don't let your shoulders slump.
5) Elevate your energy level so you are upbeat (to match the venue).
6) As you walk towards her, take note of where she is, what she is holding (e.g., the type of book if in a bookstore) so you can open making an observation.
7) Smile to her with your first sentence.

Warm-up doesn't take much time. Doing all of the above before (and as) you make the approach will greatly increase your chances of success.

The Bookstore

I was in the magazine section, walking towards the Automobile & Aircraft rack, when I saw an attractive woman looking at the airplane magazines. She appeared to be very engrossed in the magazine. I smiled as I walked to her.

Me: "This is the first time I've seen a woman in this section! Are you a pilot?"
Her: (looking up, smiling): "No, I'm not a pilot, but my friend is, I'm buying a magazine for her. She works for an airline."
Me: "That's great! But what about you – what is your hobby?"
Her: "I really like horses; I own one and go riding every weekend," etc., etc.

We conversed for a few minutes. She did not stop smiling the whole time, and was quite animated.

Analysis

I went in upbeat, got her attention, got her smiling, showed interest in what she was saying, and had a rewarding, engaging conversation.

Of course the woman's personality plays a part, but if you are friendly and engaging you can usually open up a seemingly unapproachable woman. When first starting out of course I had failures, but eventually I resolved to do the warm up exercises every time, and go into every approach with a smile. It made a *huge* difference.

You should also project an altruistic kindness ahead of your approach. This cannot be overstated – if you go into the approach wanting something from the other person, they will likely sense this, and will be less open to your advance. On the other hand, if you go in with the mindset I want to make this woman feel good about herself, or I wish to project a kind, happy aura in her direction, she will subconsciously pick up on this, and you will increase your chances of having a rewarding conversation.

Assignment #8:

Approaches Leading to Conversation

This is a natural progression from Assignment #5 in which you made small talk with strangers. Assignment #7 was designed to greatly reduce your fear of approaching women. Now try making approaches to women with the intent of holding a conversation beyond your opener. Do this a couple of nights per week after work (if places are open in your area) and every Saturday or Sunday.

Remember to keep eye contact with her, and smile periodically.

Example openers

Some openers are appropriate in one venue while being less appropriate in another; some naturally lead to further conversation, others do not.

First, here are some examples of simple openers that will *not* necessarily lead to further conversation:

Bookstore, women's magazine section: "These entertainment magazines all look the same."
Bookstore (if in the book section): "Do you like that book?"
Clothing store: "I'm slightly color blind. What color is this shirt?"
Gift shop: "Do you think my Dad would like this?"

These openers do not give the woman much to work with. Questions that can prompt a *yes* or *no* response let the conversation stall and end early and are therefore not a good route to follow. Giving her the option to say yes or no, and following up with further similar questions will make her feel as if she is being interrogated and lead you nowhere. Additionally, they force her to put in more effort. With any of the above examples there is nothing preventing the woman from saying "I don't know" then turning away and ending the conversation.

Below are some openers that have a greater chance of getting a conversation started, all of which I have used to good effect. Come up with some of your own, and write them down, taking into account the stipulations mentioned above. The point is to get the woman talking so that you are able to have a short conversation. Later we will discuss how to keep the conversation going, but if you are able to keep things moving along now, go with the flow.

> *Bookstore, entertainment magazine section:* "All these entertainment magazines look the same. Is there one you think stands out as better than the rest?"
> *Bookstore (if in the book section):* "I'm starved for some good reading. Is that book you're looking at any good?"
> *Clothing store:* "I'm slightly color blind. What do you think of this shirt with the pants I'm wearing?"
> *Gift shop:* "Hi, I'm shopping for my Father, but I don't want to get him tools this year. Have you gotten your own Dad something he really liked?"

Notice how most questions were open-ended, and would not prompt a simple yes or no answer, which we are trying to avoid. You are asking for her opinion on something, which will likely lead to a thoughtful exchange.

Questions can be your friend if they prompt a thoughtful answer. For example, let's say you had just asked the gift-for-the-father question. She might respond with a short story or anecdote about what she got her father. You could then ask if she is the person that her friends go to for gift-giving advice because she has good taste, which would further the conversation some more, and so on.

Upping the Ante with Humor

The examples above are fine for getting a woman talking, but to really put her in a good mood, use humor. Here are the same scenarios, with some humor added.

> *Bookstore, women's magazine section:* "There are so many women's magazines! I think they are instruction manuals on how women can control men, what do you think?"
>
> *Bookstore (if in the book section):* "Okay, you look smart. Is this the more intelligent section of the store?"
>
> *Clothing store:* "There are no salespeople around. If you can tell me which of these shirts look better on me, I'll give you the sales commission instead of the staff."
>
> *Gift shop:* "This gift shop is a little boring; I was hoping to get my Grandmother a Spiderman table cloth."

Any of these will get a woman to smile. She may even come up with a quip of her own *("I think Grandmothers prefer Batman!")*, a sure sign she is in a good mood and open to conversation.

A few questions are fine, but don't keep this up throughout the interaction in an effort to appear interested. Make a game about finding out about her – do a cold read. Guess where she is in relation to her siblings (is she the middle child? That means she is the peacemaker of the family). Guess if she grew up in the city or a small town.

Eight

APPROACHING in BARS & CLUBS

Bars and clubs are where you will find the greatest concentration of single women. I am not a big club guy, but I will sometimes check out a new club (or visit an old favorite) with friends. Clubs without super-loud music are more appealing because there's nothing worse than shouting yourself hoarse and not hearing the other person's reply – nothing much gets accomplished. Some larger clubs have several sections with different demographics in each, e.g., average age and music type.

In nice weather, bars with a large outdoor patio are great because of the fresh air and generally less frantic vibe, and they are a better choice if you don't dance. It pays to be versatile though, and if you can dance you'll have an easier time mingling with women if you do go to a club.

The worst thing you can do in a club is stand at the bar nursing a beer while looking around at the women. This is passive behavior that will get you nowhere. Whether alone or with a friend, try to mingle with others. It is surprisingly easy to strike up a conversation with other guys, and if it is a mixed group of men and women, talking to the guys first will make it easier to speak with the women a short time later.

If this is too daunting at first, talk to other guys that are alone. However, don't fall into the trap of talking to one guy all night just to appear social. If you strike up a conversation with another single guy, ask your new friend if he would like to be your wingman – he doesn't need to say much, but his presence may give you extra confidence when approaching a two or three set of women (wingman strategy is discussed below).

Move around and strike up conversations with others, including the bartender if they are not too busy. Don't be afraid to smile and enjoy the atmosphere.

Relaxation is key. If you are at a nightclub holding a drink, don't hold it high, at chest level. A drink can act like a security blanket, giving you something to do (e.g., sip it for an hour or two), but it also gives you something to hide behind, which people subconsciously see if you hold it high. To appear more relaxed hold it lower, close to your waist.

Here's a thought: don't drink at all. When out, cutting down on your drinking will keep your mind sharp for any conversation you have.

Here is an example of a whimsical opener, where it doesn't appear to be an opener at all. I approached a woman and her friend with, "All right, it's not working out, we need a divorce. I've decided you can keep the Ferrari, I get the Porsche."

That prompted a laugh from both women. From there I transitioned into conversation by asking them how they were enjoying the evening.

This example works best in a flirty atmosphere where people are expected to mingle. If it is used elsewhere (in a bookstore, for example) you might be judged a lunatic. Consider that the opener has a greater chance of success if it is also appropriate to the situation in some obvious way.

Enlist a Friend

If you are still tentative about going out and mingling with people in a club atmosphere, seek out a more outgoing friend to accompany you. In any case there are merits to pairing up with a friend so you can be each other's wingman. Going out with a friend that has more experience than you is a great way to acclimatize yourself if you aren't used to visiting clubs.

Since women rarely visit clubs alone, having a buddy along can make it easier to converse with a pair of women. Usually, one guy will approach the women then the second guy can enter the set a moment later, whereupon the first will introduce him to the women.

Adjust your Body Language

Remember the body language tips in the earlier chapters (don't slouch, head held high, shoulders back). If you are facing a woman completely square and looking at her constantly it telegraphs that you are completely captivated with her. It is best to angle yourself away somewhat, about 30 degrees, so you are still facing her direction but not completely framing your position to her.

Anchoring

This refers to your position relative to any stationary object in the venue, usually a wall, pillar or bar. Depending on how many people are milling about, if two people are conversing one usually has his back or side next to the bar, while the other is standing further out. It is more authoritative to anchor yourself next to the bar (or wall), and have the other person stand facing you.

If possible, after your opener and while you converse, maneuver yourself into the anchor area.

Calling women over to talk

This is a surprising fact – if you are in a club and see women walking nearby and wave them over to you, nine times out of ten they will come right over (provided you hadn't shown yourself to be passively standing in a corner for the past hour). Women like confident men, and this is a confident act on your part. Just make sure you have something interesting to say when they arrive.

You could open with the always reliable *Hi, are you having a good time?* and then transition into conversation. If you are feeling adventurous it pays to be imaginative, while talking about something they can relate to.

In our increasingly multicultural society, if you live in a big city the women you encounter are just as likely to be recent immigrants as local. Here is where talking about a universal childhood experience can be a terrific icebreaker. After waving over a pair of women, I started the following conversation:

Me: "Hey, I want to get your opinion; I just saw something on television that disturbed me. You remember Oscar the Grouch, on Sesame Street? The green furry guy that lived in the garbage can?" *The women smiled and said yes. They both had a Persian accent; watching Sesame Street as a child is near universal.*

Me: "You know how parents want kids to keep their rooms clean? Well, some parents thought Oscar was a bad influence. They said he shouldn't live in a garbage can, and that he should help keep the street clean, so he would be a positive role model for kids. Can you believe it?"

Woman #1: "That is wrong, they should leave Oscar alone!"

Me: "I know! All kids are messy. Now some parent group is telling Sesame Street to change Oscar!"

Woman #2: "Those parents are going too far, they shouldn't change the character like that; it wouldn't be the same!"

From there we chatted about different things, what they liked to do, where they were working and how they were enjoying themselves.

This type of opener is great in a bar, where people are in a good mood and are there to meet others. So the opener can be out of context, i.e., not about anything relating to the surroundings. This would not work in a grocery store, where you would need something to do with the surroundings or the woman herself.

Because the subject matter was known to them, and I delivered it as if I was talking to friends, the women were chatty, upbeat, and smiling the whole time. From here you can segue into many other topics, and also be playful as discussed earlier.

If the conversation goes well, stay in it. Some pauses are fine, but if you sense it getting stale, make yourself scarce for a while. Say you want to check on your friend or say hello to another group you saw come in. When people notice you move around the bar chatting with others it builds social proof, and your attractiveness. After a while you can return to the original pair of women and continue from where you left off.

Approaching Groups

You may feel intimidated by groups, but there are certain advantages to successfully opening a group of people. There is often at least one talkative woman in the bunch that may help carry the conversation.

Again, one of the best questions you can ask to start the conversation is, *So how do you know each other?*

Not only is this a good conversation starter (many women enjoy talking about their friendships), it can also show you who among the women are single and who the guys off to the side might be (platonic friends or boyfriends). You can approach groups solo but it is easier to work with a wingman in these situations so each of you can contribute to the conversation.

Dealing With the Jerk of the Group

Sometimes one woman of the group will be overly protective or be resentful that you've decided to break in and make conversation with them. She may give you a dirty look, or be more overt, saying something like, *What, you don't know us, go away!*

If this happens, don't turn tail and run. They can usually be dealt with, and even won over to your side. You could pay her a compliment like, *Wow, you don't take any shit do you?* and then proceed with your opener or a quick story, but directed at the other people in the group. If she persists but the other members of the group seem uncomfortable with her attitude, smile and say to the others, *Is she always like this?* then turn your attention to the more receptive members. Tune in to the mood of such a group though, and be sensitive to situations in which that one unhappy woman is prepared to escalate the situation into an uncomfortable scene. Sometimes – occasionally – you should walk away. Just remember that in this rare sort of situation, someone's unhappiness is neither your fault or your failure.

Chances are the difficult one, when she sees you are unfazed by her comments, will start to be nice and try to ingratiate herself to you. As this happens reward her with some attention – she might turn out to be a great woman after all.

Switching from the Opener to Conversation

Let's take one of my example openers:

All right, it's not working out, we need a divorce. I've decided you can keep the Ferrari, I get the Porsche.

I've used that one on occasion several times, and when done in a social setting like a party or club it never fails to get a woman to smile or laugh. But in the early days instead of transitioning into normal conversation I would continue along the divorce thread, talking about how many years we've spent together (all in fun of course), but soon I realized there was a limit to how far it could be taken before the woman would lose interest.

In other words, don't squander a good opener by milking it to death. Once she's been opened you need to transition into regular conversation. The simplest and most effective in a social setting is to ask her how she knows other people present at the gathering, or to ask if she is having a good time.

This is where your listening skills come into play. No matter what she says, you should be able to reply with a personal anecdote that relates to her comment. For example, if she says she's relaxing after a tough day at work, you could discuss work in general, how you love to recharge with a vacation (mentioning the last place you visited), and asking if she likes to travel. See how easy it is to transition from a simple topic (work) into a more exciting one (travel)?

Again, it pays to be well read, so you can relate or express an opinion on a variety of subjects. For instance, a lot of women are teachers; if you mention teaching can be a difficult job because she must be part psychologist in order to deal with children, this will build rapport with her, since you know something of her occupation.

Your Buddy – is he Friend or Foe?

Earlier I discussed the possibility of enlisting a friend to help you through approach blocks. But this entails a slight risk; your friend may be nervous or self-conscious, enough so that he doesn't help the situation. Or he may be insecure, tending to build his self confidence by making verbal jabs at others. So you may need to 'audition' a couple of friends at clubs before you find one you have chemistry with in a club setting.

You probably have one or two friends that were in a similar situation as you. You may have told them of your plan to study material to help you refine your social skills with the aim of bettering your dating life. This will elicit several possible reactions, some positive, some negative,

Scorn – *You're actually paying money for a book on how to interact with women?!?*

This criticism is hypocritical. People invest in lessons to get better at all sorts of activities including sports, public speaking, photography, dancing, and too many other interests to list here. Going further, dance lessons and etiquette coaching are examples of categories that have turned into big business, with the primary aim of helping people do well socially to make it easier to find a mate (people may tell you they take dance lessons for fun, and that may be partly true, but it's also to be more attractive to the opposite sex).

And let's not forget the roundabout way people spend money with the hope of hooking up – singles cruises, wine tasting events, specialty clubs.

And just how well is Mr. Scorn doing with women? His credit card bill likely has some charges for dating sites too. Maybe he could use some extra coaching himself.

Enthusiasm – Other friends may immediately applaud you for taking action and wish to get on board to kickstart their own social life. After a few weeks of seeing your dedication, even Mr. Scorn may come around. However some guys may jump ship after a few weeks once they realize there is no instant way of increasing their attraction to women.

Jealousy – Even enthusiastic friends can display this emotion, especially if your progress is faster than theirs. For example, I went clubbing with a friend a few times, but soon realized he would neg me in front of women I had opened.

To recap, a *neg* is a backhanded compliment, or a veiled insult, designed to reduce a person's value. Some PUAs use them on women as a tool to show they are unaffected by the woman's beauty, and to put her off balance, prompting her to try and get back into his good graces.

Though my friend had the gift of the gab, he wasn't very good at approaching or opening with women, which happened to be my strength. So in theory we made a good team. While we were talking to the women I had opened, he developed the habit of making strategic not-so-flattering observations about me, in a way that went beyond good natured ribbing.

For instance, if we were talking to younger women in their twenties (he was in his early thirties, I in my mid thirties), he would say, *You know, Chris here is no spring chicken, but his new haircut makes him look a lot younger than he is.*

Ouch! Thanks for the 'compliment,' dude. Despite any headway I made up to that point, his drawing attention to an age difference immediately put that thought front and center into the minds of the women, creating an obstacle between them and me.

At the time, I let this one instance slide thinking it was a fluke, but when he threw negs my way during the next two outings I realized that rather than focusing on positive interaction he was trying to make himself look better at my expense – a sure sign of his own insecurity and lack of confidence. He didn't seem capable of building his self-worth any other way, so I dissolved the partnership.

There are several expected barriers that you may encounter in a club, which can include the woman's cockblocking female friend, a protective male friend that you must win over and out-of-sync companions or friends who are drawing so much attention to themselves that it might become difficult for you to operate. A wingman is supposed to make the game easier, not more difficult.

Fortunately, my experience with other friends showed this guy's behavior was the exception, not the rule, so I don't want to discourage you from partnering up with a wingman. Good rapport with a friend at a club can definitely improve your game with women.

A more plausible alternative to partnering up with an existing friend is to join a PUA forum and make some connections with like-minded guys in your area. You can meet up, compare notes, go to clubs and take turns being each other's wingman, etc. This can remove some of the uncertainty of working with your existing friends.

Quite frankly, sometimes your friends hold you back. They may start out enthusiastic but often won't have the same commitment you do, so I recommend you go the online route with those that have already been studying attraction material for some time. They are less likely to quit and can be more dependable as wingmen.

Wingman Rules

Let's assume you've partnered up with a guy who's as serious as you and won't be insecure, impatient or elitist about the process. A wingman can be a great asset when in a club or if you are approaching a group of women in any setting. You can play off of each other, fill in conversation gaps, and one can work the target he is interested in while the other occupies the friends. The two of you can take turns being the one who opens the set. Here are some guidelines when you're out with a wing:

- Ideally, only one of you should approach the women at first; the wing can join a minute or two later, at which time you would introduce him
- The guy that opens the set has first choice of target (which means if you are ignoring the target at first to work her friends, the wing should know not to swoop in on her). Let your wingman know who the target is by singling her out during the introduction through making a good-natured jab; e.g., if there are three women say, "She's okay, she's okay, but this one I'm not sure about."
- Respect and agree with your wing; disrespecting your wing is unacceptable, and will backfire, lowering your own status with the women.
- When it is time to pay attention to the target, the wing should help his partner by occupying the target's friend(s).[5]

While speaking with the women, work with your wingman to praise each other's accomplishments, real or imagined, but make it something that's exciting or fits into the crowd. If you're at a bar with twenty year olds that only want to party the statement *Rob here just got his Master's degree* will probably be judged as boring, but if you are at a wine & cheese party for people in their thirties and up, it will be looked at with much more interest.

Keep in mind that if you list your own accomplishments it just comes off as bragging, but if someone else (like your buddy) mentions it, the information carries real weight.

Never Offer to Buy a Woman a Drink

Hey baby, can I buy you a drink? is the oldest cliché in the book. She (and her friends) may take advantage of the offer, but they will not respect you for it. You have rewarded them for something they haven't done. It reeks of low status on the guy's part.

If they ask you to buy them a drink, smile and refuse. Ask them to buy one for you instead, or change the subject. If they persist smile and tell them you don't like to give people handouts. This conveys dominance and humor at the same time. This may initially seem to you to be a cheap attitude, but women who ask you to buy them a drink are often just trying to find out how much they can get out of you at the bar or club. Challenging them with a little humor and authority may reset the situation in a positive way.

Nine

DAYTIME APPROACHES
street, bookstores, grocery stores

After a relationship ended, I spent a couple of weekends concentrating on approaches. Since I am generally not a night owl, I concentrated mostly on bookstores, coffee shops, and grocery stores during the day or early evening, approaching women in each. If suitable women were not to be found in one venue, I would go to the next, and then returned to the first one again sometime later. Some of the openers I used were described in Assignment #8.

If you are in the suburbs, indoor malls and bookstores are suitable for this, but if you are downtown you can usually find a vibrant shopping or business area. The best time during the week for either area is during lunch hour or just after business hours when people might do a little shopping before going home. Some areas that are vibrant during the day are ghost towns at night, or vice-versa, so you will need to get to know which areas are best at different times of the day. Weekends can be good.

The first few times you practice it helps to go in with the idea that you are not out to pick up women, but rather to practice your opening and conversational skills.

At first I wasn't very good at continuing the conversation beyond the opener, but with practice this changed and most conversations ended up lasting several minutes. In general, most of the women swung right into conversation and were super-friendly. Women enjoy interaction with confident men, and will often carry most of the conversation. Having been tentative most of my life, I was expecting to be shut down, but I was blown away by the ease with which I was able to engage women in conversation.

Of course there were some failures. Some women clearly did not want to talk (perhaps they were involved or not in the mood or simply too busy). Overall, I'd say my success rate was about 50% in finding women that were more than willing to engage in friendly conversation.

Think about those odds. Out of the women I targeted (those who were appealing to me, in my age range, and not wearing a ring), fifty percent were willing to engage in lively conversation. Not all were willing to give me their phone number or email address, but still, it is a great result, and not one that I was expecting.

One of the best lessons I learned is that you don't need to wait until you think conditions are ideal before approaching a woman. For example, back in my shy days if I saw an attractive woman in a supermarket, I would only talk to her if I could manage to be in front of or behind her in the checkout line, and even then I would hesitate and sometimes chicken out. I eventually realized you can approach in almost any circumstances, e.g., in the food aisles at the supermarket or the deli counter, which opens up the possibilities immensely.

Remember though, that the approach must be confident and the conversation interesting, ideally with some humor. If you are tense and sweaty, things are not going to happen. This is where practice helps, and using some relaxation techniques (breathing exercises, relaxing your muscles, smiling) before approaching.

When you first start doing this you will likely need to take some breaks between interactions – you wouldn't believe how much energy you expend, from being somewhat nervous and maintaining a pleasant conversation with a woman. You don't notice it at the time, but after you've been looking for a suitable woman, then make the approach, engage in flowing conversation for a few minutes, then get her email address – you may need to sit down at a coffee shop and relax for a while!

Below are two examples of approaches I have made – one successful, one unsuccessful.

Approach Example #1 – The Beach

I was rollerblading at the beach one weekend and had sat on a bench by the path to drink some water when two attractive women walked over and sat down on the next bench to change from their running shoes to their blades. I decided I was going to talk to them. I was relaxed, feeling good, and there was no rush. As they were getting settled I said, *I'll need to give you both a ticket for not wearing a helmet.* They thought I was serious at first, looking at me, then each other, then back to me, when I betrayed a slight smile. They both laughed, and we introduced ourselves, and talked for a while.

Turns out one was single and the other's husband was due to join them in a few minutes. When he arrived we all went for a skate, with the single girl and me eventually separating from the couple. We talked for about forty-five minutes. I got her number and we went out a week later.

Approach Example #2 – The Subway

I had just entered the subway train on the way to work when I noticed an interesting young woman standing next to me. She was listening to her iPod but had given me a couple of glances. One person got off at the next stop but in doing so had caught her earphone cable and almost yanked the earbud out of her ear. I smiled and said, *You almost got carried away.* It was a good opener and we talked about music for a few seconds, but then I felt some pressure to close the deal since I would be changing trains soon. I started yammering away, asking a lot of question and in doing so began to sound a bit needy. The expression on her face changed from flirty to uncomfortable, and I realized the moment had slipped through my grasp.

Analysis

In the subway situation I forgot some of the most basic rules – stay relaxed, and behave as if you are completely content with yourself, while giving the woman an opportunity to interact with an interesting guy. In the beach situation I was more relaxed and confident and it showed.

Looking at it logically, it's easy to see how and why you need to work at achieving successful approaches. Pickup is a learned art, one that requires us to employ a sincere and resolute mindset. All successful approaches will involve the following:

- Resolve (to make the approach in the first place)
- Timing (to approach as soon as possible, otherwise the moment will be lost)
- Energy (to be upbeat and friendly, without overdoing it)
- Humorous (you want to get her smiling)
- Engaging (you want the conversation to flow, rather than be strained)
- Rapport (to gain some common ground and build attraction)
- Comfort (in order for her to feel good about giving you her number)

Before you think the list is long, this is something that can be learned fairly quickly. This is why in Assignment #7 I encouraged you to make simple approaches only, without worrying about getting her number or email address (if it flows naturally into that, fine). This will take a lot of the pressure off. The goal is to get comfortable making the initial approach, while having fun learning how easy it is to talk to women. Then you can work on gradually increasing the length of the conversations.

Another Subway Approach

Public transit is a great way to meet women – I've gotten several phone numbers and email addresses from women on the subway. If the car isn't too crowded, if you see an interesting woman, try and sit close enough so that if you speak to her you will be heard.

While headed downtown I noticed a woman sitting close to me, listening to earbuds while drinking something green from a clear plastic container. It looked like some sort of health drink. Since she was wearing earbuds I knew I would need to gesture towards her to get her attention. I did a slight wave of my hand and pointed to her drink as I first spoke. She immediately removed her earbuds.

Me: "That drink looks very healthy but I bet it tastes just awful," (said with a smile).

Her: (Smiling) "It's actually not too bad, it's organic green tea. It's supposed to clear your system of toxins."

Me: "Ah. I like green tea. It's a nice alternative to the usual soft drinks, which usually make me feel lethargic afterward. The tea gives me a bit of energy without the crash."

Her: "Definitely, if I'm going to work out I stay away from soft drinks."

Me: "So you like to keep fit, that's great – me too, but I like weight training, I don't do much cardio."

Her: "I work out about three times a week, mostly cardio," etc.

Notice that I asked a couple of questions, but also made some statements about myself, and indirectly complimented her about working out. She went on to say that she worked at a gym, and gave me her card.

Tips for Public Transit Approaches

Find out what stop she is disembarking *(So, where are you headed?)* – this will give you an idea of how much time you have to build some rapport and get her number.

Mention what a coincidence it is that you are getting off at the same stop to run an errand. This way you can walk with her for a while to continue the conversation. Be sure to read her mood and reaction; you don't want to overstay your welcome or appear as if you are following her.

Add a False Time Constraint

If you get off at the same stop, to head off any feelings of unease on her part, tell her you can't talk long because you need to run that errand. Then after you have been talking for a while get her contact information.

Throwing in a false time constraint *(I'm in a hurry, so I can't talk long)* works anywhere, not just on public transit. It puts her at ease, letting her know you won't necessarily be taking up much of her time if she isn't interested. You can actually extend the conversation as much as feasible. In fact, the longer it is the better, since if it is flowing naturally and she's enjoying herself, her interest in you will rise, the time constraint will be forgotten, and she will feel more comfortable about giving you her contact information.

Indirect vs. Direct Openers

In the last few pages I gave examples of *indirect* openers, which are observational, in which you are commenting about the surroundings or making a casual (but positive) remark about the woman herself (the book she is reading, her nice jacket, the fact she appears to be the world's fastest mobile phone texter). These can naturally lead to conversation without necessarily telegraphing attraction to the woman (she can *suspect* you are attracted, but since you are being coy the stakes are lower). *Direct* openers on the other hand immediately let the woman know you are attracted to her.

Direct openers are higher risk; the woman may be very flattered that you find her attractive, but after the initial excitement of your compliment it can be downhill from there unless you are very successful in transitioning into an enjoyable conversation. For this reason I only use direct openers if there is little time or it is not feasible to employ an indirect opener.

Approaching on the Street and in Malls

This is separate from approaching in places like bookstores and grocery stores, where you have time to observe what products she is looking at or what section of the store she is in, and even in public transit, where you have some time to make an observation about her on which you can base your indirect opener.

Though in every situation I advocate approaching with minimal hesitation, the street demands the quickest action. While passing a woman on the street or in a mall you have much less time to think about the situation and must act immediately. Certainly you should observe her for a moment, but don't follow her around excessively or follow her into shops because you'll look like a stalker. Don't fixate on one particular woman – if you can't make an intelligent approach after a few moments observation, move on.

If approaching a woman you see on the street it is good to always have an ask for directions opener handy, but it helps if you are mischievous in your method. For example, glance around at your surroundings. If you are directly in front of a mobile telephone shop, ask the woman, *Hi, can you tell me where the nearest mobile phone shop is please?* She may catch on and smile at how forward you are being, but try and make it subtly obvious that you are fully aware of the shop in front of you.

If she glances at the shop then back at you with a quizzical expression, you can say, *I know, but this is a good excuse to talk to you. My name is Christopher, nice to meet you.* Smile and shake her hand. From there you can transition into normal conversation.

If you aren't ironic about the approach and simply ask for general directions to the nearest ATM, it is too easy for her to just say she doesn't know or move on after giving you the directions.

Street Approach Examples

An example of a direct opener is, *Hi, I wanted to talk to you; I noticed you have a really fantastic sense of fashion.* You are being open about why you are talking to her. You are making your intentions known (that you are attracted to her) and wish to have a conversation.

Ironically, whereas a line such as this in a bar would be sketchy at best, direct openers can work on a street or in malls. You can be even more obvious about how you are attracted to her, saying, *Excuse me, I noticed you and just wanted to say you are very attractive,* or be specific about her, such as saying, *I don't think I've seen a more gorgeous hairstyle on a woman.*

Another example would be, *I don't often see women that have it all together like you do, it's refreshing.* This serves a dual purpose. It compliments her, but also shows that you are a man of high standards.[6]

Another example: *Excuse me, but I just noticed your great sense of style, and I realized I would regret it if I didn't speak to you.*

Earlier I told you about the dangers of over-complimenting and how it can rob you of intrigue and value. This holds true when in a bar where women dress up their best and expect to be approached, or when you are on a date. However, the context in which this opener is delivered on the street ensures it will not come off as pandering, primarily because she does not expect it.

On the contrary, showing you are willing to approach a woman out of the blue with such a sincere statement will show you have balls of steel. If delivered with a confident smile this will push all of her buttons. She will feel great that a stranger noticed her, pointing out how attractive she is. Most women will be very taken with what you said.

She is likely to smile at any of the above statements. At that point, offer your hand and introduce yourself. This is a bonding experience – the handshake is a mini-icebreaker. From there you can continue the conversation by asking her what she is doing: *Are you out shopping?*

Among direct openers, my favorite is:

Hi, I only have a minute, but I just wanted to say hello. I didn't want to go through the rest of my day regretting not talking to you.

This never fails to get the woman smiling. Notice how there was a false time constraint included. This reassures her that you are in a hurry and so she won't be stuck talking to you for a long time, but if the conversation goes well, she won't want you to leave and you can then forget about the time constraint just as if you never even said it.

Physicality

Here is how a typical daytime approach may go down. If you see a woman you are interested in walking ahead of you, walk at a brisk pace to catch up. If you have not seen her face yet, glance at her as you pass by. If she isn't your type, abort. If she is, do a double take: look at her briefly, then look away, then look back at her because you're interested.

At this point, especially if you are a half-step ahead of her, she will see you without turning her head. Say, *Excuse me,* and then slow down, stopping within a couple of steps. She will most likely stop as well (if she was wearing ear buds she might not have noticed you, in which case you can wave to get her attention).

If she had been walking towards you from the opposite direction, you can stop her as she is passing you, but it may be more effective to approach from behind and then follow the tactic above, as you walk along side her. Touching, even briefly to get her attention is risky and generally not recommended (you don't want to invade her personal space or be mistaken for a purse snatcher).

Only proceed with a light touch in a safe, public environment, and you are confident she will not be startled. Never latch on to a woman – only use the tips of your fingers to lightly tap her on the shoulder or arm. Respect her personal space – give her as much of a comfort zone as you'd expect from a stranger approaching you for some other reason.

Similar to the come-from-behind approach above, she will now be aware of your presence, so while you maintain eye contact say, *Excuse me.* then slow down and within a couple of steps stop walking.

You can pause for a moment before continuing, but not more than a couple of seconds, as she will be wondering why you have stopped her. Continue with any one of the following, or make up one of your own similar statements (ideally based on truth). *I saw you back there and . . .*

 – *. . . Realized I'd regret it if I didn't speak to you*
 – *. . . Wanted to tell you what a great sense of style you have*
 – *. . . Wanted to mention how gorgeous your hair is*

In all cases, it is important that the both of you be stationary as you deliver this second statement. If she keeps walking and you follow her along as you continue and make a compliment she is likely to thank you and keep walking. Plus it doesn't look good for you, status wise, to be following her delivering compliments.

How Women React to Being Approached

As mentioned, with very fleeting encounters *direct* openers are a way to initiate conversation if you don't have time to employ an observational indirect opener.

Women usually react in one of three ways. 20% are absolutely blown away by being approached. Their faces light up with a big smile, and they often say something like, *Wow, this is such a great compliment, thank you!* The majority, about 70%, are flattered and smile.

The remaining 10% are bothered by your approach, as if it is an affront, or perhaps they view the mere act of talking with you as cheating on their boyfriend, or an invasion of their personal space. Their brow may furrow, and they will walk briskly away, giving you the brush off. This situation is obviously disappointing, but when it happens never lose your cool, just let her continue on her way. Her reaction is her own problem, not yours. Be charitable too – maybe she had some bad news earlier and is not interested in any type of social interaction or maybe she's been poorly approached by other men and just isn't open to it at that moment.

Some women think touching (even a brief, light tap on the shoulder) is an invasion of personal space. It is important to smile as she looks at you to show your intentions are friendly. Obviously you would not do this on a dark street – for her peace of mind, only make approaches in places where there are at least a few other people around.

When I first started making approaches, I honestly believed the numbers would be the reverse, with 10% being approachable and 90% giving me the cold shoulder. Imagine my surprise when I found the opposite was true – that 90% were approachable and appreciative.

I saw no discernable pattern. Extremely good-looking women were no more likely to have one or another reaction than average-looking women. Some extremely physically attractive women were wowed by the idea of being approached, which goes to show you there is not a surplus of guys out there doing this.

Even with a favorable reaction you may be tempted to try and get her number right away and get the hell out of there so you can go relax somewhere – and that's a perfectly understandable reaction, at least when you first start doing this. But be aware you will not have a good success rate if you ask for her number too soon. Don't expect to hit a home run right away. It will take many approaches to get a feel for the process.

Later as you gain some practice, make an effort to engage in natural conversation for a few moments before thinking of getting her contact information. It does not take an eternity to build a comfort level and rapport. Conversations can last anywhere from about three to ten minutes, or longer. In those few minutes a lot can be accomplished. You can find out things you have in common, get her laughing, and hopefully get her intrigued and interested in seeing you again.

Do Not Eject from the Conversation

When first starting out, your conversations with women will probably be short. If the conversation doesn't flow naturally or if there is a pause, you may get nervous and will be tempted to excuse yourself. This is natural, especially early in the process as you are learning. Your mind will be preoccupied with thoughts on how to keep the conversation going, but ironically this can cause the conversation to stall.

Each time this happens, instead of kicking yourself for bailing, review the circumstances and think about what caused you to eject. Most likely you ran out of things to say, and she was waiting for you to continue the conversation. I'm sure afterward you can think of many things that would have kept the conversation going, but the trouble is, how do you do so in the moment when you are with an interesting woman?

The obvious solution is practice, where you will slowly gain the ability to think on your feet and say things that will advance the conversation (e.g., using *Yes, and,* see the section on Improv).

Be sure to listen to all of her responses, so you can build upon them. For example, if you ask her where she's off to and she replies, *the health club,* you can respond by praising her for keeping in shape and ask if she runs, cycles, rollerblades, etc., and then mention something similar you do.

Ejecting too early is a form of self-sabotage. Stay in the conversation until she excuses herself, or you feel confident enough to get her contact information, but continue talking to her for at least a few moments after you get her number (maybe she isn't in a hurry and would open to go for a walk or coffee right then and there). The more you practice, the longer you will be able to keep the conversation going, and the more likely you will generate some rapport, so she is comfortable giving you her contact information.

She will eventually do much of the talking

As you gain experience the situation gets easier. It's true you will need to start the conversation (use any of the example openers in Assignments 7 and 8, or make up your own), but once the conversation starts many women will open right up and carry much of it for you.

The odds of women carrying the conversation go up if you open with a topic that is interesting. If you only ask her the time, the conversation will naturally end quickly unless you can hook her with something else. The humorous openers that I suggest in the assignments are designed to lead in to natural conversation.

If the conversation drags a bit, remember, pauses are not the enemy. Maintain eye contact, make a positive observation about her or what she is doing.

Note that for whatever you say, you must maintain strong body language and use a strong voice (appropriate for the venue). If you deliver your dialog as if you are apologizing for disturbing her, she will immediately pick up on this and be more likely to end the interaction.

Developing your listening skills will help you in all your interactions, making you appear interested in the other person, something everyone appreciates.

Reducing the Flake-Out Factor

Ah, the flake-out. A common phenomenon to all potential dating avenues, from online dating to cold approaches, is the Flake-Out Factor. This is when you get a phone number or email address and your communication attempts are not returned, or her communication stops after one or two exchanges. This happens to everyone, so you should not feel discouraged when it happens to you.

There are a number of reasons for this:

- She's thinking she doesn't know you well enough to continue, or her initial enthusiasm has waned over time (this is known as buyer's remorse – what seemed like a good idea at the time is no longer okay)
- She might have a boyfriend she didn't mention, and while flattered at the attention you gave her she realizes she doesn't want to jeopardize her current relationship
- She may not be feeling adventurous (women can be as conservative or shy)
- She might be busy, and any initial excitement she felt at the prospect of going out with you has faded as her lifestyle gets in the way
- . . . And other reasons, known only to her

The number one cause of the flake-out is that not enough comfort and rapport was generated before asking for her contact information. In other words, you probably bailed out of the conversation a little early, or you started to appear too interested and needy (or nervous, as you ran out of things to say), causing any attraction you generated to wane.

The number two reason is that too much time has elapsed between the initial and subsequent contacts. If you have a great ten-minute conversation and get her number, but wait five days before calling, chances are she will have forgotten much of what you talked about. Contact her the next day, or no more than two days after the initial conversation.

Better yet, during the initial conversation work in some interesting event you are going to that evening, and call her up later asking if she wants to go. If you make it a group thing (your friends and hers) she will be more likely to say yes.

By increasing the number of approaches you make you will improve in all areas. As your approach anxiety lessens and you gain more practice, your conversational skills improve and you will more easily establish rapport, which in turn will reduce the flake-out rate. Most important, your own increased comfort level will lead to longer (and better) conversations with women. A woman's comfort level, and her attraction to you, are paramount.

This gets much easier with practice. As we learned in earlier chapters, people love to talk about themselves, so if you make a few observations about her and ask a few key questions, she will likely open up and carry much of the interaction. However, you must be able to kickstart this interaction from scratch, and provide her with a reason to keep talking. As long as you make interesting observations and comments, she will more than likely respond positively.

Success Rates

Many women in a bar or club will be single and expect (or want) to be approached by a confident guy. Daytime approaches sometimes present more of a challenge because a lower proportion of the women you see will be single. Or, they may be single but not expecting to be approached at that moment (but some will be pleased at the prospect).

Therefore, your success rate in a bar may be slightly higher, especially if you are able to approach groups and have the benefit of a wingman.

Then again, few women dream about meeting their soul mate in a bar. More likely they fantasize about meeting their next boyfriend during a chance encounter, such that may occur in a grocery store, coffee shop or bookstore. Since I rarely go to clubs most of my own success has been with daytime approaches, usually without planning ahead, as I talk to women I happen encounter when out and about.

If through practice you are able to offer confident, engaging conversation and build rapport in the first minutes, the odds of getting an email address or phone number is approximately one in five. Of those, approximately four in five will flake out. In other words, of five women that gave you their contact information, one will be willing to communicate extensively after the initial interaction, so the true success rate is one in twenty-five.

This is only a rough estimate for when you are starting out. If you naturally take to this exercise and become good at building rapport, you can improve those odds. If you have some trouble building a comfort level the flake out rate might be higher. However, for the moment let us assume for every twenty-five women you approach, one will be willing to engage in extended conversation after the initial contact, leading to an actual date.

When you think about it, those are good odds. You're approaching women cold, out of the blue, some of whom have boyfriends (though no ring), or some other personal reason for not dating, and approximately one out of twenty five will go out with you. These are women you are choosing, those whose physical appearance, age, style, and demeanor appeal to you, which is not always the case for women you meet through online dating sites.

Speaking as a former sales rep, I would need to call approximately 250 potential customers (on average, in the field I was in) to get one new client. So if I'm willing to make 250 cold calls to get one additional client, I'm certainly willing to make 25 approaches to get one date, or make 250 approaches for dates with ten women I find attractive.

Let's say you're like me and you aren't satisfied with the bare minimum of getting one date from twenty-five approaches, and you want ten dates. How long will it take you to approach 250 women?

You should be able to approach twenty-five women per week without much difficulty, provided you are disciplined and do this in a busy mall or street shopping area. You could have at least one date (that's date, not phone number) per week, and twenty-five dates over the span of six months.

This number does not take into account any online dating you might be doing. Factor in those and you can increase your date rate even more.

Keep in mind you don't always need to go out with the idea of making "X" number of approaches every day. As you get better at this, you will find yourself approaching women even when you had not planned on doing so, wherever you are: waiting in line at a take-out restaurant, walking on the street on the way to the gym, and any number of other places you visit or frequent.

Limiting Beliefs with Approaches

If you are reluctant to start making approaches to women, it may be due to some limiting beliefs you have about the process. Below are some common ones.

Conditions Must Be Ideal

Most guys think conditions must be ideal before contact can be made with a woman they see on the street, bookstore, grocery store, or some other public place:

- She must be rooted in one spot for an extended period, so she is less likely to move away when approached
- She can't be distracted, wearing earbuds or typing into her BlackBerry
- She must demonstrate through her body language that she is receptive to someone talking to her

Some of the conditions you may invent are so broad, they will never be achievable and you will end up always finding a reason why every woman is unapproachable. The reality is, you can make approaches to those browsing in bookstore or grocery store aisles, in a mall, or on the street, even if she is walking at a brisk pace.

Fixating On One Woman

If you do not have a lot of dating experience there is a tendency to fixate on one woman to the exclusion of others. This one-itis (another PUA term) is bad. First, it blinds you to the other possibilities out there. Second, your dream girl at the office (or wherever) may not feel the same way about you. One of the reasons we want to talk to a lot of different women is precisely to learn how to quickly determine who might be interested in us and who is not interested in us. About the only way to do that is to talk to them.

Fixating on one woman tells you more about yourself than anything else – and little of it is very good. Talking to a lot of different women on the other hand, will reveal a lot of good things about yourself to the women you meet, and perhaps just as important, to you. Confidence and overcoming shyness comes in part from experiencing the great variety in our world and from interacting with the great variety of women.

If your dream girl dominates your every waking thought, you will not be thinking clearly about proper interaction with her and will make multiple mistakes, such as trying to time your lunch room breaks to coincide with hers and other stunts that will become obvious to her over time, making you appear needy or even creepy. Your infatuation will reduce your attractiveness, and result in a complete transfer of power from you to her. When she senses this, her interest in you will be eradicated (if there was any to begin with).

Only slightly better is concentrating your efforts on a select few women rather than practicing on as many as possible. Many aspiring pickup artists study the material thoroughly, thinking they have all the knowledge necessary to attract the one or two women per year they develop a crush on. The result is they fail to develop their practical skills, and become very discouraged if they fail in their attempt to attract one of those few women.

For any of the exercises to be of any genuine benefit they must be practiced as many times as possible on as many women as possible.

The Age Question

Let's say you are looking for women that are younger than you, either to keep the option of having a child, or simply because you are attracted to younger women. But you are concerned they may think you are outside of their age range.

If you ask random women the ideal age range of a potential partner, they generally state that they are looking for someone the same age as them up to about seven years older. Some women say five years older is the upper cutoff, while others as high as ten or twelve years (it depends on the individual).

That does not mean women are not open to dating outside their stated age range, even the ones that state five years is their upper limit. Charisma and personality can trump age, up to a point.

This is where meeting someone in person – either at social gatherings or making cold approaches – has an advantage over online dating sites. Some sites have search filters women can set with regard to age (so men over the limit can't message them), and even if they don't use the filter, if a 30 year old sees a message from a 42 year old guy, depending on her preference she might delete the message before reading it, deciding 42 is too old before even responding.

These disadvantages are drastically reduced in the real world because, even if she consciously thinks a twelve year age difference is too much, once she is engaged in interesting conversation the age factor may fall by the wayside.

Everyone has their limit, of course. If you are sixty and regularly hitting on a twenty-five year old women, you would likely need to be an outstanding individual with several compensating factors thrown in (e.g., fame and lots of money) to have any chance of success.

Likewise, if you look old for your age – have long grey hair, out of style clothes, and are in poor physical condition, your chances of success with younger women are reduced, even if you are charismatic.

But for more reasonable age gaps, you can maximize your potential by projecting your best image, which includes keeping yourself in good physical condition, dressing well and carrying an air of confidence.

I have an acquaintance that is a couple of years older than me, and for as long as I can remember he always looked a bit older than his actual age. He would dress very conservatively, never changed his hairstyle (which was now going grey), and wore very generic eyeglasses. Then one day I saw that he had changed his appearance by dying his hair and wearing contact lenses. Although his clothing and hairstyle were unchanged (except for the dye job), he now looked years younger. I think he should have gone further, changing his wardrobe, but this was a step in the right direction.

The Personal Attractiveness Question

You may be reluctant to approach women because you view yourself as unattractive. You're unhappy with your looks. As mentioned earlier, when researching this book I spent some time on a shyness support group site. I was struck by how many guys were in a state of despair and resignation at what they felt was their ugly appearance. Some of these individuals described themselves as below average, perhaps a 3 on a scale of 1 to 10.

Some of these men could not be convinced that making an effort to better their appearance through dress, hairstyle, etc. would make any difference in attracting women. Because they thought they were naturally unattractive it meant that no external changes would make things better.

Of course attractiveness is subjective, but we've all seen what we would think of as unattractive people, at work, in shopping malls, or on the street. However, the next time you are out, take note of the next unattractive person you see.

Chances are, they have poor posture, are not walking with confidence, are wearing unfashionable eyeglasses or clothes (or worse, their clothes are ill-fitting, worn out or stained), or have an unflattering hairstyle.

Next, take note of everyone you see that is well dressed. If a person is well dressed with great posture and a neat or trendy hairstyle, you are far less likely to think of them as unattractive, no matter what physical imperfections they have. At worst, you would likely say they were average, which is not a bad thing. Now, if they had confidence and charisma, they would be more attractive still to anyone they talked to.

Let's say you are a self-described 3-out-of-10 with some of the negative pitfalls we've been talking about. If you change your walk and posture (as described in the *Develop some Style* section), keeping your shoulders back, head high, and avoiding constantly looking at the ground, you can literally gain a point or two, transforming yourself into a 4 or a 5 with these changes alone.

Changing your hairstyle and clothing to something more modern and flattering can gain you another point (all these improvements are more effective when they are made together).

Finally, if you smile more, greet people with enthusiasm, and can carry a conversation, you have just added another point. This is an example of being your best self, someone that will no longer have any disadvantage when attracting women.

Guys who realize this and put in a genuine effort to better themselves are putting themselves on the road to personal and professional success in every area. Men who are not open to this reality will not make any progress.

Ten

THEORY versus REALITY

Up to now I've given you some real-world examples of approaches and their results. Hopefully once you have finished the book you will then start venturing out and practicing the assignments, which is crucial if you are to move forward.

With some self-instruction material, some guys are able to interact with women in a meaningful, productive way (as in having an interaction that leads to a date), while others gain a false sense of security, thinking that the act of reading a book or watching a few YouTube videos on the subject will automatically transfer PUA skills into their consciousness.

Some men buy several books and DVDs, but then don't go out into the field and practice what they have read or seen. They may encounter a mental block that stops them from taking the first steps. Or they may think they don't need to practice, instead believing that if the right woman comes their way they will be prepared. Unfortunately, it is not as easy as that.

Albert Einstein is believed to have said, *"One definition of insanity is doing the same thing over and over again and expecting different results."* If you read and understand some new theories but at the same time fail to change what you are doing, don't be surprised if you continue to fail.

Implementing new social skills takes time and commitment. If you have been used to praising women all of your life, it is a big change to switch over and start playfully teasing them. If you are exceedingly grateful for any show of affection they give you, it may go against your instinct to do a little push-pull in order to remain a challenge to them. So you can see how making these basic changes will require some effort and experimentation.

Here is an example of theory versus real-world skill. As a kid, I loved planes and wanted to be a fighter pilot. This dream stayed with me to early adulthood. I went so far as to get the required physical before joining flight school, but unfortunately found that I'm slightly color blind; at night, green lights appear white to me. Unlike some other eye problems, this cannot be corrected, and even though I can see most colors under most conditions, this is a deal breaker for a lot prospective pilots because they're restricted to non-commercial, daytime flying. So I chose a different career path.

However, up to then I had read about the theory of flight, studied up on control surfaces, used flight simulators on the computer, and paid attention when my licenced pilot friend went through his pre-flight checklist before taking us up in his single engine Cessna.

In a pinch, I might be able to take off and land a small plane, despite not having any experience doing so. If my friend had some sort of unknown medical condition and suffered a seizure while in level flight I might, repeat – *might,* be able land us in one piece. Likewise, if my woman and I were being chased by a bloodthirsty gang through the jungle and the only way off the island was a seaplane (one that was warmed up and in perfect condition), I could probably get us to safety.

But under normal conditions, if I gave it a try would I do well? Probably not. Despite having a good grasp of the theory, I do not have the practical experience of flying a plane. Under pressure I would likely forget items on the checklist. I might use too much (or too little) flaps during takeoff or landing. I might over-rev the engine. I might overcorrect a banking turn, sending us into an uncontrollable spin.

So, despite having an enthusiastic interest in planes, my lack of practice (not to mention the fact it is illegal to fly without a licence) stops me from taking a light plane out flying. Learning how to fly a plane takes time. There is classroom instruction, exams, practical time behind the controls. That's why there are no *Get your pilot's licence in 20 minutes!* courses out there – it just isn't feasible.

And that is also why you should be suspicious of any PUA material that claims you can get a woman into bed within 20 minutes. As mentioned earlier, the more serious PUAs don't make such claims anyway, preferring to have the person build up their social confidence with the goal of improving their social and dating life.

Short Term Excuses can turn into Long Term Failure

If you have gone out with the intention of making a few approaches, you should be given a thumbs-up for at least getting out there, but realize you must go further and make the leap to *regularly* talking with women. Some guys read everything they can on PUA techniques and then hardly make a single move. I call these guys Barstool Analysts. Even though you might be going out frequently (whether to a bar or not), if you have been voraciously reading PUA material for the past several months or more but don't approach women with any regularity to put the theory into practice, you are a barstool analyst.

This is a terrible situation because on the one hand these guys are painstakingly preparing themselves for a situation they want to be in, while at the same time ensuring they never enter into that situation for which they are expending so much effort because they perpetually feel they are unprepared, and must continue studying before making a move.

Another common excuse is to claim that the women they encounter are not the *right type,* e.g., the woman might be dressed in a way you aren't used to, looks like she might be high-maintenance, or otherwise seems unsuitable. Appearances can be deceiving. Some of the most snobbish-looking women are super friendly once you get them talking. Others act aloof because they themselves are nervous, but if you give them a chance their true personality may come out.

Encountering women that are apparently not your type should be the exception, not the excuse. You shouldn't be looking for a female clone of yourself – people have differing backgrounds and interests. For instance, if you are a Country & Western guy you may not feel at home in a lounge that caters to urban professionals, and vice versa. If that's the case, start out in places where you feel most comfortable. But it pays to be versatile, so unless you can't live without your cowboy hat, why not try a place you wouldn't normally frequent, to open up new possibilities?

The best way to learn and change your perspective on something new is to start small. But starting small also means taking action within a short amount of time and building your skills. The barstool analyst justifies his inaction by trying to learn everything possible on the subject of attracting women, and is constantly preparing for his Big Day, when he will finally feel he has enough knowledge to approach women he sees and sweep the woman of his dreams off her feet.

There are two possible outcomes to this scenario. One, he will never feel he has enough knowledge, and will amass ever more PUA material, until finally he gives up and finds something else to occupy his time, never really having done anything the books have taught him.

Or, after reading volumes of material he finally goes out, but expects to immediately hit the jackpot on his first few tries, only to see himself crash and burn due to lack of actual experience. He then gets depressed at how difficult this approach business is.

Success under these conditions is unrealistic. Would you be an expert tennis player by only reading books and watching tournaments on television before your first game? This stuff takes constant practice, and you need to accept and deal with some failures before you get better.

These are limiting beliefs about both yourself and the women you will be approaching. Some nervousness and disappointment is inevitable. You must push through it and take action, not use it as an excuse to do nothing. The warm-up exercise can help here, as can re-doing Assignment #7 in which the stakes are low (not expecting to converse for very long).

Another type of barstool analyst is the one that feels conditions are never right for him to be making approaches. Thought patterns such as these can occur daily:

- **I need to be in the right mood to approach.**
- **When I'm in the mood to approach, there are no suitable women around.**

This is a falsehood, so don't let it become your normal thought pattern. This can also turn into a medium-term to long-term condition where the man thinks he is too busy at that moment or believes things must improve in his life before he can start making approaches.

Here's how that scenario might go:

- First three months of inaction: I just got a new job, and I'm stressed out at the new responsibilities so I'll start making approaches after I get used to my new job.
- Three months later: I'm really out of shape due to my desk job. What woman would want to date a guy that's let himself gain 10 lbs over winter? I'll start making approaches when I get into better physical condition.
- Three months after that: I'm renovating my basement so it can be rented out as a separate apartment, therefore I'm too busy and stressed with that right now; I'll start making approaches after I get a renter.

Or substitute an infinite number of additional stress or lack-of-time factors. You can see how new excuses replace those that have gone stale, and how what was supposed to be only a few weeks of inaction can literally turn into months or years.

There is always something going on in life that interferes with their dating efforts. This is rationalization to deal with the fear of getting out there and talking to women. It makes the person feel better about their inaction, but it also means they are making zero progress. In fact, some guys spend far more time and energy analyzing why they aren't making approaches than actually going out into the field.

Everybody has changes and stresses in their life, yet we carry on and get things done. We're still able to interact with coworkers, shop for groceries, go for a drink, research deals on our next car purchase, etc., despite being busy and having the stress of what's going on. Yet when it comes to dating or simply making small talk with women with the intent of building attraction and getting contact information, these excuses are deemed to be all-encompassing and insurmountable difficulties that interfere with his *emotional preparedness*.

This is nonsense. Unless you are undergoing some debilitating medical treatment or dealing with the recent death of a loved one, there is no typical life event that would make it impossible for you to talk to women you encounter. If you are able to get through life's everyday hurdles you can do this too. It takes literally a couple of minutes to mentally prepare yourself, and only a minute more to make an approach. Do the warm-up exercise. It can be something as simple as taking a deep breath, exhaling, and asking an interesting looking woman about the location of the nearest coffee shop.

That's it – that's all it takes to start making approaches. Do this a few times and it gets much easier. Practice Assignment #8, using that section's example openers.

Too many guys over-think the situation. When they see an attractive girl they stop and think about how they don't feel the vibe is right, or all the possible negative outcomes and what her rejection of him will feel like. So they stand there paralyzed, taking no action. Had they approached without hesitation with an example opener they would instead have experienced a feeling of elation at the accomplishment, even if they didn't get her number.

But I'm not a barstool analyst, you may be thinking. *I had a great conversation with some women at the bar on my birthday, so I'm getting out there and interacting with people. One of the women even gave me her number.* When was your birthday? A few months ago? Did you and the woman end up going out on a date? No. Have you had any more great conversations with women since then?

Oh, you're renovating your bathroom, and are stressed out because the new sink was cracked and its replacement is on backorder. But you'll start making approaches after that is taken care of. Oops, now your dog might need an operation, and you're worried about it. Right. Well, at least you have the memory of that great conversation you had five months ago to keep you going. I'm sure your friends love it when you reminisce for the umpteenth time how great that conversation was, and how into you the woman seemed, even though you never saw her again.

Rather than take action some people continue to think of their situation as unique, or they claim that once the latest issue is settled (e.g., they lose 10 lbs or buy that new car they've been thinking about) they will be in the right frame of mind in order to devote the energy to the business of approaching women. If this was only the latest in a long line of rationalizations, you can bet the next excuse is just around the corner.

If you experience these thoughts yourself you must recognize they are *limiting beliefs* that are preventing you from taking the needed critical steps in your development. The first course of action is to stop making excuses, and start implementing the advanced assignments immediately.

As we've seen before, the lead up to a good approach is quick and simple, not complicated and time consuming. When taking a break from work, talk to the woman in line ahead of you at the coffee shop. Are you taking public transit to your job? Talk to the woman beside you, or the woman that you've noticed that gets off at the stop just before yours.

Approach Anxiety

For most men, women are the ultimate prize. Show some guys a beautiful woman and they may turn into jelly from a mixture of desire and fear of rejection. The more the man is attracted, the greater these feelings, and the greater the chance of failure.

It's ironic, but it's also a fact: the more you want something, the greater the chance you will blow the opportunity to get it. This is why you must lower the stakes when it comes to making approaches. Think of your first approaches as reconnaissance missions to gauge the reaction of the women. As I've mentioned in previous sections, the vast majority of women out there are flattered when you approach them and are willing to talk, provided you are fairly confident.

Some approach nerves are good. A bit of nervousness is natural and shows you that you are about to do something that can potentially reward your action.

All accomplishments of any significance induce anxiety or nervousness. Are you nervous going into a final exam? Of course, but once you finish you have a sense of euphoria at accomplishing a task that was worthwhile (i.e., the exam was one more step towards successfully completing a course or getting a university degree).

Are you good at an individual or team sport, enough so that you enter competitions? I'll bet you were nervous before the big games. Maybe you even felt like throwing up before getting out onto the field. But you played anyway, and if you won the game you felt great afterward. Even if you lost, you probably had a rewarding sense of satisfaction at getting as far as you did.

You are nervous at making approaches because they are worthwhile activities that can reward you, but entail some risk (rejection). You must understand though, that even if you are rejected, what have you lost? Typically the woman remains polite and moves on. She doesn't laugh and point her finger saying, *Hey everybody, this loser just approached me! Come join me in mocking him!*

In reality the risk is so low as to be almost nothing, especially if you do this in an area you don't normally frequent. As you make more approaches you will realize this, and think to yourself, *Why the hell didn't I do this earlier,* especially as you get better and start getting phone numbers.

To avoid losing your nerve, don't go in thinking that the woman is destined to be your wife and you must get her phone number. Instead, think of her as one among many dozens of women you will be approaching, and simply go in to exchange a few lines of conversation, and then exit (see Assignment #7). Lowering the stakes can take a lot of the pressure off.

Once you make that first approach, you will feel great! Now you deserve a large latte or new DVD for a job well done. Rewarding yourself like this after your first approach (and then say, every five approaches thereafter) will set a pattern of success in your mind, making it easier to forge ahead.

Later as you get used to approaching you can work on extending the conversation and getting her contact information.

Here's a little tidbit of information: most seduction masters admit to having some approach anxiety, especially if they have been away from the game for a while. But after the first one or two approaches are behind them they are back in form.

Approach Skill Plateaus

Learning and mastering any skill involves peaks and valleys as you progress. I've noticed this in virtually everything I've studied: golf, improv, dance lessons, Tae-Kwon-Do, and weight training.

There is the initial barrier as your mind and body are confronted with something new, so at first you struggle. Then you are able to make quick progress (up to a point) where you feel great about acquiring this new skill. But then as you make the effort to reach the next level you may get impatient and start to make errors and some beginner mistakes which cause you to regress slightly. This leads to frustration. At this stage some people quit. But if you are not a quitter you regroup, refocus, refine your technique, and start to progress again.

Depending on the activity there may be several plateau cycles, but one thing is certain: if you stop practicing for an extended period (as little as a couple of weeks), your skills will degenerate and you will need to work extra hard to get back into form. Patience and persistence are key.

Additionally, if you've had some success but then seem to fail often (you either fail to engage the woman beyond a sentence or two, or you get her number but she flakes out later) your mind starts to work against you as the fear of rejection and failure starts to take over. In this case it makes sense to start again at a lower level, perhaps by re-doing one of the earlier assignments where the stakes are low and you're not expected to number close.

Analyze What Went Right & Wrong

After a relationship fizzled out I decided to return to making direct approaches, after not having done so for a few months. Despite having success previously, I made a few rookie mistakes, and it took me a few days of consistently approaching women before I got back into the groove, getting phone numbers.

It's best to read this section after you have already completed the assignments, because I don't want to give the impression that there are so many ways to go wrong. It's true there are many mistakes to avoid, but that's the way it is in everything. If you handed a golf club to a guy that has never golfed before, don't expect him to drive the shot straight down the fairway; it's more likely he will hit it into the woods. It will take practice and dedication for him to get his stance, grip, balance, swing and follow-through correct, at which time he will have some success. The more you practice worthwhile activities, the greater the rewards.

The key here is to gain knowledge and experience. When starting out you will likely make mistakes, but as time goes on, so you get closer and closer to your goal. I wouldn't have much respect for a new golfer if he hit his first dozen balls into the woods and then stomped off in a huff, saying golf was *too hard*. However, I have the greatest respect for people that stick with it, and improve every month. Besides, practice is part of the fun.

It will help to break down the approach issues into steps, so you can work on refining each of them separately.

Hesitation

Hesitating too long before making an approach works against you in several ways. First, the longer you wait, the greater the chance she'll leave the area, the friend she was waiting for will show up, her phone will ring, or she will otherwise become unavailable.

Second, the woman may notice you orbiting about, trying to get up your nerve. This will lead to her feeling uneasy, so she will likely try to avoid you, or reject your eventual approach.

Last (and most important), your hesitation will allow self-doubt to creep in. The longer you wait, the harder it will be to walk up to her and start a conversation. It is best to approach with in a few seconds of seeing the woman, no matter the venue. Take a brief time to do the warm-up exercise and then go for it.

Opener Delivery

The delivery of your opener is very important. You need to smile and speak with a strong, confident tone. Don't speak as if you are sorry you are bothering her. Speak as a confident guy that has a lot to offer.

If your voice or body language is meek you will sound as if you are asking permission to talk to her, which makes it easy for her to shut you down. Confidence makes all the difference. Go into the interaction thinking you are the desirable one (without being cocky). In fact, you can have what may be considered a goofy opener, but if it is delivered with confidence it will have a greater chance of success.

Additionally, if you have gone through a few approaches, after a while your energy may wane and you may be just going through the motions, where you appear insincere or your voice has lost the energy it once had. Make an effort to project your voice with confident energy and a smile, even if you are tired.

Don't keep walking after opening

If approaching a woman who is walking, after you have delivered your opener slow down and stop walking within a couple of paces. As the woman sees you slow down and stop she will usually stop with you, at which time you can transition into conversation.

If you keep walking along side her, or if she doesn't stop and you then catch up to her again and walk along with her, it can be unnerving to the woman and you will appear to be pandering. If she doesn't stop or leaves, just forget about her, regroup, and concentrate on the next prospect.

Again, the delivery of your opener is important. If you are energetic and charismatic in you opener the woman is more likely to stop.

Speak Confidently and Slowly

After the woman stops it is time to transition into conversation. You may be nervous and thus tempted to speak quickly, with lots of hand gestures, eyes darting about. The more relaxed you are, the more relaxed she will be. Don't forget that pauses are not the enemy; they can make you appear thoughtful (as long as you don't force her to carry the conversation). Keep your voice tone a bit lower than normal (which will counteract your natural tendency to speak in a higher tone if you are nervous).

Keep your eyes on hers, and don't forget to smile. Keep your hand and arm movements to a minimum.

Don't ask for her contact information too soon

Remember, after your opener you need to transition into conversation and develop rapport and comfort. If you are nervous and can't think of anything to say you will be tempted to ask for her number too quickly. If you do this to early, she will likely decline and excuse herself from the conversation.

With each approach, try and extend the amount of time you spend in conversation. Some women won't want to be kept long from whatever they are doing, but others will be happy to stop and engage in conversation with a confident man.

As your conversational skills improve you will discover ways in which to get a woman laughing and comfortable giving you her contact information.

Also, once you have her contact information stay in the conversation for a bit rather than exit right away. This shows you are genuinely interested in her as a person.

Solutions to Approach Roadblocks

You may be having trouble with the initial approach. If so, enlist a friend to help you out. Have him watch discreetly in the distance, or better still, work with you as a good wingman. You will be more apt to actually make an approach if you share the effort. Once you have completed this exercise, repeat it the next weekend, and the one after that. Soon you won't need to strike up any kind of partnership with your friend because your skills will have developed to the point where you can go out alone, anywhere, and approach women.

If you need to start out small, let's say by only asking a woman's opinion on something (see my examples on bookstore approaches), that's fine. By not being required to escalate and get her number you will be taking a lot of pressure off yourself. But at some point you *must* escalate. Keep pushing the boundaries and increase the conversational time.

Remember to follow the advice on personal grooming, and especially bettering yourself by taking general interest courses, specialized arts courses, and joining charitable groups you are interested in. Over time these activities make you a more well-rounded person, giving you more things to relate to and talk about.

Putting yourself out there does not come naturally to most men at first. This book is designed partly as a reference manual, and should be referred to multiple times after first reading it. To be successful in improving your social life you must not only comprehend the material, but live it, employing the instructions within on a daily basis.

Once you have made a few successful approaches, you must follow up regularly in order to keep the skill alive. You are embarking on a behavioral change which requires constant repetition and reinforcement to become natural.

Failure to do this will result in a skill regression. If you have made good progress over a few weeks do not decide to take a month off.

Always be *On,* and remember your goal. You must become a man with easy-going confidence. A man that does not get flustered when circumstances are not perfect. A man that can engage almost anyone in conversation. A man who women want to be with.

Before your Date: Phone Game

No matter the circumstances leading up to getting a woman's number, you need to reestablish comfort over the phone.

To ensure you're still in her mind after your initial meeting, call her the next day. If you have trouble getting through to her (e.g., the phone always goes to voicemail), keep the message short and upbeat, and say you will give a call back later. If she does not return your message, call again the next day, then two days later (if necessary). Three phone calls is my limit. If she doesn't return your third call, assume she is not interested and move on.

The first time you catch her on the phone don't ask her out. Keep the conversation upbeat. Relay anything interesting that happened to you during the day, including people you met. This lets her visualize your interesting social life. Ask how her day went.

The expression *always leave them wanting more* is common among standup comedians. Leaving on a high note, while the audience is at the peak of enjoying the set, keeps the future demand for the comedian high.

This is also true with phone conversations. Always be the one to end it, and on a high note.

If you sense a mutual interest, call again a couple of days later with a proposal to go out. Dinner, or even just a coffee, is not a good first date because the two of you will be sitting across from each other, and it will probably feel more like a job interview than a date.

A better first date is one that involves walking, at a crafts show, an outdoor music festival, a park (especially during a special event), or even window shopping in a trendy part of town. After you've done this for an hour or so the initial jitters will have passed, then suggest the two of you go to a coffee shop to recharge.

Eleven

WHEN on a DATE

To Compliment, or Not to Compliment

You can make one or two compliments about her appearance per meeting (e.g., *You look great in that outfit),* but that's all. Any more than that and you will be seen as pandering.

If things are going well, it is a good idea to throw in a few role reversal lines. These not only can get a laugh, but it will show you're sophistic-ated and that you understand the dance that is human mating behavior. An example would be (if she paid for your coffee) *Don't think that pay-ing will let you have your way with me later!* (say it with a smile).

Who Pays for the Date?

Given that most women have decent jobs or careers the question of-ten comes up on whether the man should always pay for the date. If you asked her out you should definitely pay, even if she offers to split the bill. If you go on multiple dates with a woman and she eventually suggests an event or dinner, the chances are good that she will offer to pay, rational-izing that the person that takes the other one out should foot the bill. If you insist on paying in this instance she may get offended, thinking you don't respect the fact she has a job and can afford it.

With most modern couples it is not unusual for the woman to pay at least 20-30% of the time, if not closer to 50%, or to split the bill on occasion. Don't let her do this more than half the time or you may look like a cheapskate. Also, don't be a coupon clipper, always looking for special deals when going out, and don't pull out your calculator when figuring out the tip (do it in your head) – leave 15% tip (or 20% if the service was good). Don't be afraid to splurge on a nice meal every once in a while, but if money is tight, look for things to do that are free such as outdoor music or art showings, and cooking dinner for her at your place (provided you have already gone out a few times and she is comfortable with the idea).

Touching

Each woman has a different definition of what constitutes an appropriate touch from someone she just met. It also depends on the venue – are you in a dance club where if a woman turns to you for a dance you can put your hand on her hip without even a word, or are you in a mall where any physical contact beyond a handshake would be inappropriate?

In most situations it is fine to shake her hand during an introduction while smiling and looking into her eyes. This immediately breaks a barrier and makes it a little easier to touch her later on. If you are able to get her comfortable and laughing she may touch you playfully. If so, it can be considered a green light for you to do the same (but don't overdo it by touching her at every opportunity).

If you are moving to a different venue you can touch her back briefly to guide her in the direction you want to go.

These are all harmless gestures but at the same time when paired with good conversation build familiarity and attraction. Gauge her touch and her reactions to your touch before deciding to escalate. If the encounter is going well and there is obvious flirtation and attraction going on you can increase the frequency (e.g., touch her wrist, stroke her upper arm) but only if the attraction is mutual. If she stops touching you it may be an indication you have gone too far, in which case rein it in. If she starts touching you again, you can start touching her again.

When to Kiss

If the conversation goes well and the woman seems into you, hope-fully you have escalated through increased touching, such as holding her hand, or placing her hand on your leg while resting your hand on hers.

If she doesn't pull back and continues to show you signs of interest – such as looking at you intently, smiling, playing with her own hair (or yours), returning your touch – it is time to give her a kiss.

Kissing her cheek is safer for the initial kiss. Don't ask to kiss her; wo-men like kisses to be stolen. Sometimes while on a date if I feel things have been going well I'll ask her the time and play a little trick:

Me: "What time is it?"
Her: "It's 9:30."
Me: "It is? Well you know what that means."
Her: "What?"

Then I lean in and kiss her. It usually works quite well, provided I didn't misread the signals. There is always the possibility of kissing a little too soon, but if she is uncomfortable, back off for a while, then try again about a half hour later. Usually she will be more receptive. Don't French kiss the first time, unless she decides to do so during the kiss.

I've had women comment the next day that they were impressed with my boldness. Then again, a few said that I kissed them too soon; it de-pends on the woman.

Getting Mixed Signals

Sometimes you can get the signals wrong and even waiting an addi-tional half hour doesn't cut it. Or, she was sending you signals of interest, but her strict upbringing or religion takes over and she shuts down. With these women it may take a few dates before you can progress to a kiss. But if you are able to generate comfort and attraction a woman usually won't object to a kiss on the first real date.

When in doubt, make an attempt to escalate to the next level. If you are too tentative women loose interest and put you into the friend zone.

A Lesson on Restraint

Women (including female friends) can give mixed signals. They say guys are notoriously bad at interpreting signs of interest, one way or the other.

I had a strange but intriguing experience with an attractive female friend whom I met in acting class. She was auditioning for the part of a stripper in an independent film, and asked if she could practice lap dancing at my place, with me as the customer. She also asked me if I would accompany her to a second audition with the director later that day (she wasn't happy with her performance in her first audition). Since I'm always willing to help out a friend, I agreed (in this case hesitating less than a microsecond before giving my answer).

Once she arrived I put on the music she provided while she changed into her costume. I sat back on the couch and she started dancing in front of me, getting closer and closer, as a real stripper would.

Significantly, she had a live-in boyfriend. When I asked why she wasn't practicing with him she said he didn't have the patience for it, and she was more comfortable with *me* in this situation. This was getting interesting.

She added that she needed to polish her performance for her call back audition, and she trusted me to help her get through an embarrassing process. I could understand her reasoning. I imagine most women would be a little uncomfortable gyrating in front of a committee of strangers during an audition like this.

I was in a quandary. She was gorgeous, and was so close to me I could feel the heat from her body. At one point I put my hand on her hip. I was thinking of making my interest more overt, but since she was a friend and legitimately needed to practice for the audition, I decided to err on the side of caution and just let her do her thing, allowing her to progress the situation if she wanted it to go further. Alas, she kept it professional.

Later as she repeated the performance with me in front of the director, he remarked that she appeared far more comfortable than before. My friend thanked me and we parted ways. She got the part.

This was several years ago, and I have since wondered what might have happened had I been more assertive. But it came down to trust and integrity – she was a friend asking me for a legitimate favor, unusual though it was, and any moves I placed on her would probably have back-fired, and her trust in me would have been compromised. if I were to do it over again, I would change nothing about the interaction at my place.

However, if she didn't have a boyfriend instead of us both going to our respective homes after the audition I would have invited her out for a drink or something to eat. It would have been a great opportunity to talk with the goal of building attraction without compromising our friendship (especially since after we finished the acting course we didn't see each other much).

But she *did* have a boyfriend, and ultimately that was the deciding factor in my inaction. Aside from the ethical issue, you don't need to complicate things by going after a woman who is involved. Even if she is the one to initiate a romantic involvement, it is far better to concentrate your efforts on single women. Who wants to be the *other man,* someone who will never be number one in her life?

Twelve

ENSURING YOU
GET a SECOND DATE

If after completing the early assignments you still feel nervous, realize this is normal and you're probably better in social situations than you were before. Your progress may have taken some time, but is still measurable. You are likely able to go out more often, see more people, talk more, and feel less pressure in social contexts. The exercises and assignments are working, but you may need to repeat some of them to move forward.

You've put the theories into practice and gotten a few dates with different women, either from an online profile, meeting someone at work or through a friend, or from one of your direct approaches. A major sticking point might be that you rarely get a *second* date with the same woman. On the other hand the women in whom you are *not* interested want to see you again.

A reserved man's nature can make him appear nervous or boring. The courses and social outings I advocate in the earlier chapters of this book are designed to address the social anxiety you feel when in the presence of others, but it may take extra effort to overcome the unease you feel with a woman, especially if you are attracted to her.

Keep challenging yourself through attending community events, enrolling in courses that force you to interact with classmates (female and male), take on work that gets you meeting clients, and seek out ways to polish your presentation skills. As we well know, shyness is difficult to overcome and so you must put yourself into challenging social situations as much as possible.

Again, even if you have attained a good comfort level in professional and social situations, dating may be another matter. If women you find unattractive are calling you for a second date, this is actually a good sign. It shows you can be an interesting person when the pressure is off. After all, if you aren't attracted to her you aren't nervous.

I recognize that trying not to blow it with an attractive woman can be nerve-wracking. The suggestions below are designed to counteract that problem.

Join online dating sites, date as much as possible

Although I advocate making cold approaches, dating sites and speed dating events can be a good way to practice. But don't have any expectations of finding The One, although if it happens that's just great. By going on multiple dates with a different woman each time, you will lessen the anxiety that you feel, especially if you don't expect fireworks.

If you are extremely attracted to the woman, there is a greater chance you will forget everything you've learned about being confident and un-affected, and so you will come across as needy. Re-emphasize the basics, including having assertive body language and not agreeing with abso-lutely everything she says.

Don't put her on a pedestal

Cultivate the attitude that women need not be put on a pedestal. Wo-men are not mysterious, powerful creatures that you must do your best to impress. Most of them are nervous about dating too, and are hoping for a decisive man to get them through an uncertain evening. Think of what you do differently with a woman you don't feel attracted to – you are relaxed and not trying to attract her.

Develop the ability to make a woman feel good about herself, but without pandering. Ask about her family, her schooling, and plans for the future. Don't praise her more than once or twice. The more you praise someone the less value it carries, and it can make you appear weak.

Questions versus Statements

A few questions are great for getting the ball rolling, but don't keep this up throughout the date in an effort to appear interested. Too many questions feel like an interrogation and can be fatiguing to the listener. It can also make you seem desperate, as if you can't think of anything interesting to say.

Make a game about finding out about her – do a cold read. Guess where she is in relation to her siblings. Is she the middle child? That means she is the peacemaker of the family. Guess if she grew up in the city or not.

Questions are useful if they can lead to a deeper conversation. For example, you could say, *Lots of women are charming on the outside, but what makes you unique? What sets you apart from other women?*

This not only opens the court to conversation, it also demonstrates your values. You are looking for an exceptional woman, and asking that particular question prompts her to sell herself, to list her best qualities.

After she answers, there's a good chance she'll turn around and ask the same of you, so make sure you can give a substantial list of your great qualities.

Make statements, such as how much fun you had last weekend hanging out with your friends or family. Toss in a story about your young cousin or niece, and how you enjoy spending time with them. This builds value and allows you to show your vulnerable side.

Don't talk about yourself all evening

Are you talking too much about yourself? Even if you are not normally a braggart, the temptation exists to qualify yourself by mentioning your high educational level, your nice car with the fantastic sound system, and how great you are at the latest online game.

Unless the conversation stalls, it is better wait for a woman to ask you about your job or hobbies instead of volunteering that information right away. When asked, don't be reluctant to answer in an effort to appear mysterious; the fact you didn't volunteer it is mysterious enough.

And as covered in the Art of Conversation section earlier, it helps if you add anecdotes or additional interesting information or experiences about your job or hobbies rather than just listing them.

Don't tell your date about your problems

Stay upbeat and positive as much as possible throughout the date. Even if she tells you a gloomy story, don't launch into a monologue describing your horrible lot in life or the boss you hate. Be sympathetic but also try and cheer her up, accentuate the positive things she may be experiencing.

Stick to relating positive experiences you've had, and the fact that you like your job (even if you don't). I'm not suggesting you lie all night or be unnaturally happy, just that you let the optimist in you shine through. Show her you can't be put in a bad mood or be embarrassed easily and can laugh at yourself.

If you are at a restaurant treat the server with respect. I was once on a date with a woman that was rude and sarcastic to the server. I'm not sure if she was trying to impress me or not, but it was a complete turn-off, and the server didn't deserve it.

Mind your manners

It's sad to say that some people, especially guys, have poor table manners, e.g., talking while chewing their food, checking out other women, wearing a cap while at the table, pointing at others, staring at other diners, answering their phone or texting, butting into conversations at adjacent tables, tapping or drumming on the table, holding and using cutlery incorrectly, reaching across a date's plate instead of asking her to pass something, over-salting, splattering ketchup, not cupping his hand when squeezing lemon or lime into his drink, ducking toward the plate at every bite, slurping soup. There's more and it speaks to inattentive upbringing by his parents. If you are uncertain about your own habits it will pay to get a book on social etiquette or consult a lifestyle coach, both of which can help you in ways beyond teaching you simple table manners. Below are a few basic pointers.

Set your phone to Silent, and don't check for messages every five minutes. Let calls go to voicemail. Don't text during your date. If she starts texting when you are talking to her, stop talking until she puts the phone down. If this happens several times sooner or later she will get the message and will put the phone away. If she doesn't put the thing away, say to her, *Wow, that must be really important.* Hopefully she will take the hint. Don't be personally offended either. Smartphone use, texting, tweeting and mobile email are so pervasive, and apparently addictive in some respects, that a lot of otherwise terrific men and women have developed terrible phone habits.

Don't look at every attractive woman who walks by. It may be tempting to let your eye wander, but it is completely rude not to have eyes only for your date. Even if you think she won't notice, women have a way of knowing if you keep checking out that hot woman at the next table.

Dress appropriately

Don't be lazy about what you choose to wear. While it is true that confidence and personality are the most important factors that women weigh when deciding if they want to see you again, unless you have the charisma of the Dalai Lama and Batman all rolled into one, dressing like a slob will work against you.

Dress appropriately for the venue and don't be afraid to class it up a bit. Consider wearing a nice jacket and shirt. Jeans are okay if worn with a jacket and the establishment doesn't have a anti-jeans dress code.

Consult the earlier section on Style, which covers these topics and more, including hairstyle and accessories. Most important, wear decent shoes – women notice!

Memorize a favorite story

Everybody has a story to tell, but calling it up when under pressure can be difficult. Your mind can go blank when you're looking for something to say. This is one reason I am such an ardent advocate of improv courses - they get you accustomed to thinking on your feet.

During a relaxing moment at home, think of something funny or interesting that recently happened to you or someone you know. Or go further back, to a college prank, a childhood adventure or practically any story that has amused listeners in the past. Most of us have a story we've told many times. Write it down in detail, then think of a title. Create a separate section with the title and two or three key points so that if you were to glance at the title later you will recall the story in its entirety.

Good storytelling takes practice. If you aren't a good storyteller, practice and record yourself on video. Pretend you are talking to a friend, and use good voice tone, pauses, facial expressions and moderate body movements or gestures that might aid the story. View the recording and take note of what you're doing wrong. Are you talking too low? Too quickly? Stammering? Fidgeting nervously? Shifting from foot to foot? Is the story too long, loaded with unnecessary detail? If so, cut it down to a manageable length, no more than a couple of minutes.

Record it as many times as necessary to eliminate any negative habits. Practice again before your next date. Enter the title of your story and two or three key points into the Memo app of your mobile phone.

When on your date, if the conversation lulls, try and work in your story. If possible don't check your phone notes in your date's presence; this shows poor etiquette. Wait until she leaves to use the washroom or excuse yourself for the same reason to refer to your phone notes.

This plan will be more effective if you have several stories to choose from. This way you have a better chance to match the story to the personality of the woman or the direction the conversation has gone so far. For example, if one story is a little racy you must be sure the woman will not be offended by it.

Memorize some routines

Scripted routines are touted by some pickup artists as a way to increase a woman's interest in you by tapping into her imagination. Some people may say routines are deceptive or a crutch, but if used *sparingly* they can be effective conversation aids without making you come across as insincere.

When you think about it, routines are used whenever the goal is to get (and keep) someone's attention. Comedy talk show hosts warm up the audience with a stand-up routine. Would viewers prefer it if David Letterman was completely honest and told them he was only being funny to get them to watch his show, and proceeded to just say whatever popped into his head, instead of employing writers? Dave's a sharp guy, but nobody can do that and be entertaining night after night.

The television show is a willing partnership. We enjoy watching, and if we didn't we'd tune out. In a sense, a date is no different. Each person is trying to win over the other, and the pair that succeeds will go on to a second date. Those that gain a subsequent date do so in large part by saying the right things at the right time.

I'm not saying your entire date should be scripted; far from it. Once you get more comfortable with women you should dispense with routines altogether. But if you have a couple of amusing routines at the ready you can help turn the tide to help improve a date that isn't going well.

In general, women love astrology, anything to do with the supernatural, and taking personality tests. There are many examples of personality tests on every PUA chat forum. One of the first ones was the Cube Test, of which many variations exist. This is where you ask the woman to visualize a cube in the desert, and then ask her questions about it. From her answers you are able to form a conclusion about her personality.

You'll be totally making up your answers. If you do it well she will be fascinated by the process. Who cares that it's all nonsense? It's entertainment, but you don't need to tell her that!

A typical cube test might go like this:

You: "Hey, there's a great test that can tell a person's personality. Would you like me to test you?"
Her: "Sure, go ahead."
You: "Okay, close your eyes and imagine you are alone in a desert; the sand is smooth, the sky clear and blue, and there isn't another person around. Now visualize a cube in the desert. Can you see it?"
Her: "Yes I see it."
You: "Good. Now tell me, is it resting on the sand or suspended in mid air?"

Her: "It's about ten feet in the air."

You: "Terrific. Is it large or small? Solid or transparent?"

Her: "It is about the size of a car, and transparent."

You: "Wow, that's interesting. All right, now I want you to imagine a unicorn. Got it?"

Her: "Yes."

You: "Tell me where the unicorn is in relation to the cube. Is it on the ground away from the cube, or somewhere else?"

Her: "He's inside the cube."

You: "Amazing, all right, you've completed the test, now I can tell you how you did.

At his point she will be rapt, waiting for the results of her test.

You: "Because your cube was suspended in the air, it tells me you have a very active imagination. You like to daydream a lot, and sometimes that gets you into trouble."

Keeping the analysis broad like this yet positive almost always gets the woman to agree.

"Also, because your cube was transparent it means you wear your heart on your sleeve, but since the unicorn was inside the cube, it tells me you are an enigma. You are sometimes misunderstood. In fact some people when they first meet you might think you are a bit cold, but that is not the real you. It also tells me you really need a creative outlet, otherwise you feel a bit trapped."

As long as you keep the analysis positive and general, most women will agree with your assessment. Had she originally said the unicorn was on the sand, you could have remarked she has a grounded personality and that her friends come to her for advice. If she said the cube was opaque, you just as easily could have concluded she has a strong personality.

The whole exercise has a way of building rapport between the two of you. Keep in mind that you need to emphasize the visuals and the peaceful nature of the imaginary desert. This will put the woman into a nice, comfortable place. Reach your conclusion clearly and with conviction.

Relay the test with a flourish. Inject a few *Wow, that's interesting* or *amazing* comments. Don't cut the experience down to, *Imagine a cube and a unicorn in a desert, where are they in relation to each other,* then giving an assessment after her first reply. The exercise is supposed to be a creative effort. The sample script, above, is just a starting point.

Cocky + Funny = Second Date?

This has almost become a cliché, but it is largely true. If you can be humorous and a little teasing towards the woman it will increase the likelihood she will be attracted to you. This is effective only if you don't misread the situation – many women are turned off by overly cocky men who don't know when to be serious.

For reserved people the idea that they can be easily cocky may be too far outside of their comfort zone to be viable. But you can still prod a woman with gentle teasing, which can be very disarming and flirtatious if done right. If you find the conversation lulls a bit, say something like:

I usually don't date women from the wrong side of the tracks, but I'll make an exception in your case.

If up to now you have been having a serious conversation and she hasn't seen a glimpse of your sense of humor, be sure to deliver a line like this with a slight smile so she knows you are joking. She will probably smile back and tease you with something like, *Oh really! Are you from the snobby part of town?*

You can continue the banter by remarking that you *Like to help underprivileged people,* but know when to switch gears and stop teasing. If done intelligently this technique is great for building rapport, but you wouldn't use such a line on someone who actually has money problems.

You can also be playful; sometimes the most childish games are the most fun. For example, you can challenge her to a thumb war. If you haven't touched her yet she may be surprised, but you aren't going for romance at this point (though this exercise makes it easier to build romance later on).

Imagine her surprise when you reach across the table, take her hand and say, *One two three four I declare a thumb war!* and proceed to pin her thumb under yours. Even if she's never played this game before she'll catch on quickly and play along, most likely smiling the whole time. Be gentle with her hands and fingers.

If you are older you can still do something playful like thumb war. When we're on a date, what was funny to us as children is often funny again. Happy moments such as these have a way of helping us relive our childhood.

If you have been completely serious up to now this works great to break any remaining ice. It shows you are fun guy that can let loose sometimes, and it will reveal a new facet of your personality she might not have seen.

Don't try and convince her to see you again

If you haven't dated much in the past there will be an acclimatization period in which it takes some time for you to be confident and at ease enough so that a mutual attraction develops. In other words, you may need to go through many dates with different women before you start to get comfortable.

Until then, if your date gives you the *let's just be friends* or the *I didn't feel a connection* speech, just accept it and move on. I know this can be a blow, especially if you were very attracted to her, but ironically it is this very attraction that may have worked against you.

If in your star-struck state you had forgotten some of the basic rules and engaged in nervous conversation rather than easy-going, humorous teasing and were too quick to compliment and give her your undivided attention, you would have thrown away any value, and would not have been a challenge.

You may be tempted to use logic to try to convince her that you were a little tense and should be given another chance. Or you may list all your wonderful attributes and remark that she is being too quick to write you off. It will not work. Once a woman has made up her mind that you are not boyfriend material (even if you are), no amount of reasoned argument will change it. Be courteous and finish the evening positively and with a good attitude. Don't pout. Bow out gracefully and with dignity.

When it comes to dating, we make decisions based on feelings, not logic. If she decides you are not the one for her, no matter the cause, you could recruit a team of the world's greatest thinkers and philosophers, led by the spirit of Socrates, and they would still fail to change her mind.

She doesn't want to see you because you did not ignite attraction. In other words, you were lacking the right balance of humor, confidence and intrigue. These are the things you need to work on in order to make progress.

However, if she is in your regular social circle all is not lost. If you become a more grounded, charismatic guy, don't pander to her, and continue to date other women, she will notice your increased social value and may eventually send you signals that she's interested. If she does, *don't drop everything and run to her.* That's the attitude that turned her off in the first place, so you must strike a balance between showing her attention and not pandering to her, and have the ability to inject some humor in your interactions.

Keep your place clean

Eventually after you gain enough practice and a comfort level with dating, things will go well, and you will bring a woman back to your place. In preparation for this, keep your living space clean, especially the bathroom. You may have become desensitized to the dirty dishes in the sink or last year's tax receipts strewn all over the corner of your dining room that you haven't gotten around to cleaning up, but she will notice the mess. Likewise, she will be turned off by a dirty bathroom mirror or mould in the shower.

Show a woman a clean apartment or house and she'll be more comfortable, and therefore more apt to be affectionate with you.

You Will Succeed

Consider the exercises in this book to be part of a mission you *must* accomplish. The alternative is unthinkable and unacceptable – only minor improvement that really doesn't get you out of an empty, lonely existence.

Because you are more self-aware than the average person, you can push through the barriers that stand in the way of your success. You are not going to read one chapter in this book and then put it aside for a month, or blame society for all your ills. You will not fall into the trap of understanding the material, but not putting it into practice, like the other people that meekly give up on whatever self-help program they enter.

If you still lack confidence when talking to people, re-read the early chapters, so you can identify and eliminate your remaining Limiting Beliefs. You won't be able to change your entire outlook on life (and yourself) in one go. It will take repetition and commitment. It is expected and necessary to live the changes, which will allow you to move down a new, more exciting path.

The success rate for people like yourself will be better than average, because you won't read this book as a novel, forgetting the messages it contains a week after you finish it, or letting it gather dust on the bookshelf after it's read once. Reading this book cover to cover is just the beginning – taking action, doing the assignments and referring to this book dozens of times is what will move you forward.

Final Assignment

Finishing this book is the first of many steps you will be taking. There is no quick fix. You must be making the effort at all times, referencing this text when appropriate to help you forge ahead.

One of my favorite movies is *Glengarry Glen Ross*. The plot revolves around four real estate salesmen, their manager, and the corporate type from downtown that comes by to give them a motivational speech, which verges on cruelty. The film is relentless in its gritty portrayal of the macho, sometimes sleazy salesmen and the lengths they will go to make a sale. If you haven't seen it, rent it.

Glengarry Glen Ross is wildly entertaining and sometimes over the top, but the guy from downtown has a message for his salesmen: this month's sales contest will earn the winner a Cadillac, a set of steak knives for the runner-up, and the rest will be fired.

In his pep talk he gives one central message: ABC

– *Always Be Closing*.

That's the mindset you should have: *Always Be Improving*.

Are you feeling braver than that? How about: *Always Be Approaching*.

Do you see an interesting woman at the grocery store? *Approach*.

See some interesting people at a party? *Approach and be friendly*.

Is there a single woman at a party you want to meet? *Approach*.

Your final assignment is to spend a few minutes, right now, entering into the calendar/reminder function of your daytimer, BlackBerry, iPhone, iPad, Outlook or smartphone the following entries, with an audible or visual reminder to prompt you to read the entries at the scheduled time.

Set the following entry at one week after first completing this book:

Have I completed the first few assignments outlined in From Shy to Social? *This is a reminder to myself to not let the book sit after only one reading. I'm going to re-read the assignments, then start and complete them ASAP.*

Set the following entry at one month after first completing the book:

By now I should have finished half of the assignments in From Shy to Social, *including those on improving my attitude and appearance. If I'm not referencing the book at least twice a week, I will start doing so now.*

Set the following entry at three months after first completing the book:

By now I will have taken some of the specialty courses suggested in From Shy to Social, *and repeated the early assignments many times, while working towards the more advanced assignments. If I've gotten sidetracked, I vow to get back on course* **immediately***.*

Set the following entry at six months after first completing the book:

I have read key sections of From Shy to Social *several times, and completed all the assignments, repeating some of them. I have taken more than one hobbyist course, and plan to take more right away. I have made real progress and* **I will not quit***.*

So there you have it. I have given you the *Plan*. You have the *Motivation*, and will make the *Time*, putting in the *Effort*. You will succeed, and create the rich social life you deserve.

Review

Assignment # 1: Online Contributions (p. 48)
Become a 'star contributor' and reviewer on enthusiast forums.

Assignment #2: Voice Projection & Telephone Clarity (p. 54)
Working on your voice, telephone manners.

Assignment #3: Improve your Look (p. 65)
Personal grooming, style, maintain a confident physical presence.

Assignment #4: Saying "Hello" to Strangers (p. 74)
Say hello to as many people as possible during your daily activities.

Assignment #5: Short Conversations with Strangers (p. 76)
Practice small talk every day with people you encounter.

Assignment #6: Enroll in Special Interest Courses (p. 77)
Take several consecutive courses with an arts theme.

Assignment #7: Approach 50 Women in 10 Days (p. 104)
Remove your nervousness by engaging in very short conversations with many women over just a few days.

Assignment #8: Approaches Leading to Conversation (p. 139)
Extended conversations with women using your listening and conversation skills.

Notes

1 (p. 11) - Randolph M. Nesse, Is Depression an Adaptation? ARCH GEN PSYCHIATRY/VOL 57.

2 (p. 22) - Michael Pilinski, Without Embarrassment: The Social Coward's Totally Fearless Seduction System.

3 (p. 30) - Mihaly Csikszentmihalyi, Flow: The Psychology of Optimal Experience. Harper Perennial Modern Classics.

4 (p. 94) - Harasty J, Double KL, Halliday GM, Kril JJ, McRitchie DA (February 1997). "Language-associated cortical regions are proportionally larger in the female brain." Arch. Neurol. 54 (2): 171–6.

5 (p. 150) - Mystery, The Mystery Method. New York: St. Martin's Press.

6 (p. 158) - Michael Marks, The Dating Wizard.

Bibliography

Csikszentmihalyi, Mihaly. Flow: The Psychology of Optimal Experience. Harper Perennial Modern Classics, 2008

Ellsberg, Michael. The Power Of Eye Contact. Harper, 2010.

Lowndes, Leil. How To Talk To Anyone: 92 Little Tricks for Big Success in Relationships. McGraw-Hill, 2003.

Machowicz, Richard. Unleash The Warrior Within, 2nd Ed. Da Capo Press, 2008.

Markovik, Erik von. The Pickup Artist: The New and Improved Art of Seduction. New York: Villard, 2010

Marks, Michael. The Dating Wizard, 2003.

Mystery. The Mystery Method. New York: St. Martin's Press, 2007.

Nesse, Randolph M., MD. Is Depression an Adaptation? Arch Gen Psychiatry/Vol 57, January 2000.

O'Connor, Joseph & Seymour, John. Introducing NLP: Psychological Skills for Understanding and Influencing People. London: HarperElement, 2002.

Pilinski, Michael. Without Embarrassment: The Social Coward's Totally Fearless Seduction System. Michael Pilinski, 2002

Strauss, Neil. The Game: Penetrating the Secret Society of Pickup Artists. HarperCollins, 2005.

Strauss, Neil. Rules of the Game. HarperCollins, 2009.

Acknowledgements

Editor: Howard Carson
hcarson@gmail.com

Manuscript consultant: Nate Hendley, Toronto-based freelance writer and author
www.natehendly.com

Cover design: Sonya Thursby
www.opushouse.com

Web sites

Kateryna Spiwak, dating & relationships expert
www.datingessentials.com

Dale Curd, Counselor, men's issues expert
www.dalecurd.com

Other books by Sunbow Press

We Have Seen The Enemy and They Are Odd

A present-day alien invasion. Among the public there is apprehension, terror and panic as the invaders quickly reveal their intentions. However, the aliens are not quite what they claim to be.

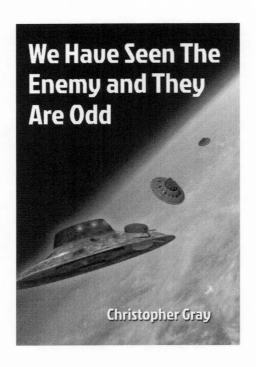

"In forty years, the aliens had not revealed their physical appearance, nor volunteered any information about their home world, despite many requests that they do so. As he signed the report, Colonel Gibson realized something surprising. Two generations had grown up not having known anything of a world without Merlins. For over half the living population of earth, they had always been present..."

Humor/Satire
eBook ISBN 978-0986836466
Print ISBN 978-0986836473

1440

Made in the USA
Lexington, KY
20 January 2014